# Let Us Pray

# Let Us Pray

## A Plea for Prayer in Our Schools

## William J. Murray

*William Morrow and Company, Inc.*
*New York*

Printed in the United States of America


2 3 4 5 6 7 8 9 10

Produced by K&N Bookworks/Designed by Jaye Zimet

# [ACKNOWLEDGMENTS]

I would like to acknowledge the dedication to this project of my wife and office manager, Nancy M. Murray, my staff and the services of writer-scholar Kenneth Ross and the research team of Patrick Ross, Lisa Brand Agnew and Jane Glickman. My special thanks to all my friends in Congress without whom this work would have been impossible. I would also like to thank Billy Zeoli, Steve Zeoli, J. R. Whitby and those at Youth Films who have supported this effort. A documentary film based on this book is available from Youth Films by calling 800-253-0413.

We will miss forever Dr. Jimmy Morgan, who joined his Creator for all eternity just days prior to the publication of this work.

# [ C O N T E N T S ]

# What This Book
# Is About

The desire to pray is a natural human instinct. Prayer is the primary medium through which all people, past and present, have expressed their relationship to the divine. It is at the heart of every religion, a universal act in which expression is given to one's deepest feelings. All religious faiths agree that prayer is central to human life. Buddhists, Christians, Muslims and Jews assert that it gives order and meaning to their religious experience. William James said that without prayer, there can be no question of religion.

The move to restore prayer to our public institutions has been associated with conservative clergy and some conservative politicians. And it is true that the main impetus to renew a spiritual and moral vision for America has come from these groups. My own roots are deep within the conservative movement for smaller government. However, it is a mistake to label this a partisan matter. School prayer is a cultural marker, signifying an issue much larger than itself. Every citizen is paying a high price for the elimination of prayer and spirituality from public life. This has been widely recognized, even by liberal politicians. Leaders across the political spectrum have called for a spiritual renewal of American society and the family. School prayer is a step in that direction. It is my hope that this issue will unite people from every political and religious affiliation. Prayer is a universal human phenomenon, an inextinguishable impulse in time of need, a fundamental component of every religious tradition.

We live in a society that officially bans prayer in its public schools and most other public institutions. What are the implications of this indisputable fact? Does it matter? We can still pray in our homes and in some private institutions; in churches, synagogues and temples. In fact, we can pray just about anywhere as long as those prayers are silent ones. Has anything really been lost? I believe, and I think history suggests, that something exceedingly important *has* been lost. To those who would ban prayer in schools and public institutions, I ask the following questions: Is it possible for a nation to maintain a corporate sense of morality without public prayer? Is public prayer, so ancient and traditional in the life of nations, obsolete? Should a tradition at the center of institutional life for millennia be legislated into extinction? The answer to these questions is, in my opinion, a resounding no.

I believe the issue of school prayer exists in a context that transcends the merely political or sectarian. Institutional prayer has not been the victim of any single factor. Prayer has succumbed to the inexorable movement of our nation away from the sacred.

Secularism infuses our entire culture. It affects everyone. It is a movement in which many have participated, wittingly and unwittingly. It is true that a few individuals and organizations have worked diligently to eliminate every vestige of religion from public life; among them, militant atheists and various fringe groups. But they are only bit players in a larger drama. No group or organization could have accomplished this on its own. Our public officials, educators, judges, bureaucrats, and many of our clergy, have aided and abetted the process. Secularism has insinuated itself into every aspect of our culture.

Few institutions have escaped this long and progressive disease. The sacred has been systematically rooted out of our public, scientific and intellectual establishments—but not completely. Prayer is a resilient concept that shows up renamed in a dozen "scientific" euphemisms from "consciousness effect" to "telekinesis." At an Ivy League university, researchers tested whether people could influence physical events by thinking about them. Their conclusion: "Human consciousness establishes a 'resonance' with the physical world that can reduce some of the randomness around us." Recognizable in this technobabble is an insight already realized by every major religious tradition millennia ago: Prayer affects the material universe. The ancient vocabulary of faith has been replaced by the lifeless terminology of the scientist, a lexicon devoid of any moral vision, ignorant of history, bereft of tradition, discontinuous with the past. A strict avoidance of any reference to every concept that could possibly be construed as religious is a hallmark of our scientific, educational and public institutions.

But there are other issues we must consider. In addition to the process of secularization, school prayer has been subject to much misunderstanding concerning the historical and contextual roots of religious freedom and church-state separation. Even religious people confuse or exaggerate the degree to which the founding fathers intended to separate religion from government. As we will see, they certainly did not intend to remove prayer from public institutions, the workplace or schools. Both sides of the school prayer debate have appealed to the same sources in support of their arguments. Unfortunately, the founding fathers have been invoked more than read. Jefferson's ideas concerning the role of religion in education, for example, have seldom been discussed. The historical, religious and philosophical factors that influenced the framers of the Constitution have received scant attention in the popular press. But these issues are not difficult to understand. The First Amendment has a history, a context. The controversy over school prayer cannot be understood apart from a knowledge of that context.

While the authors of the First Amendment were still alive, and for generations after, religion played a vital role in America's public schools and in government itself. The historical record is replete with examples of how religion was at the heart of American education. School prayer was taken for granted. The vast variety of religious sects and denominations disagreed about nearly everything, but agreed on one principle: the importance of a moral and religious education. A decentralized federal government left education in the hands of local authorities, and schools employed a wide variety of curricula. Local control guaranteed that the content of religious education in any particular school represented the prevailing sentiments of the community in which it was located. Disagreements sometimes arose, but for the most part children received an education without controversy and free of coercion. The founding fathers believed that a moral education was essential to the maintenance of the republic, and most communities put that belief into practice. As Alexis de Tocqueville observed in 1830, every child was "taught ... the doctrines and the evidences of his religion, the history of his country, and the leading features of its Constitution."

As time passed, attitudes about religion and education changed. People remembered and continued to affirm the Bill of Rights, but gradually forgot the history responsible for its creation. Separated from any remnant of state religion or persecution for generations, the original reasons for the establishment of the First Amendment slowly diminished in importance. As church-state issues were debated and eventually litigated, the First Amendment began to be reinterpreted on the basis of new criteria. As we shall see, through a series of landmark cases, its meaning and intent was modified and extended by successive generations of Supreme Court justices. They didn't always get it right. What began as a guarantee that the state would never establish or support any particular church or enforce any official doctrine—as had been the case in England—developed into a legal principle that threatened to prevent the expression of all religious sentiment within public schools and institutions altogether. The original First Amendment guarantee to every citizen, of the right to free religious expression without consequence or state interference, was transformed. This remarkable process, which took many years and many court decisions, turned the First Amendment inside out.

The 1963 *Murray* v. *Curlett* school prayer case, in which I was the plaintiff, was the culmination of many years of drift away from the original intent of the First Amendment. My mother, Madalyn Murray O'Hair, and the militant far left atheist movement she represented, sensing the direction of court sentiment, provided the last small push needed to remove prayer from our public schools. This milepost on the road toward the complete secularization of American society was reached through an unlikely series of events and an even unlikelier cast of characters. The people, personalities and events that led up to the 1963 Supreme Court decision prove that history is far more interesting than fiction. Hollywood's best screenwriters could not have invented more colorful characters. Confrontational and self-promoting, my mother orchestrated a series of events that focused national attention on herself—and me. Her actions were ostensibly issue centered, but in my opinion were more personal and psychological. In the end, however, her motives mattered little—she had succeeded in tipping the balance. School prayer was weighed, found wanting and eliminated.

Prior to 1963, my mother wanted to live in a Communist nation where God was never mentioned. For a long time she tried to defect to the Soviet Union for one simple reason: The Soviets had long ago banned religion and prayer from public life. But she eventually decided to stay. She stayed, not because she changed her mind about religion, but because the nation itself changed. Against history, tradition and the intent of the nation's founders, church and state became divorced, not merely separated. In an ironic twist, the United States, founded on explicitly religious principles, adopted a policy similar to that of the former Soviet Union, a nation founded on a Marxist ideology that was explicitly antireligious. Madalyn Murray O'Hair, angry, flamboyant, single-minded, took credit for an antispiritual revolution that had consumed America.

The character of public education in America has changed dramatically since 1963. I attended school in Baltimore, Maryland. Baltimore was a very different place when I lived there. In fact, there are really two Baltimores: the Baltimore prior to 1963–the city my mother hated–and the Baltimore of today. When I went to school, there were no metal detectors at the door. Students were never searched for guns, and I cannot remember a single shooting or murder on campus in my entire time as a student in the Baltimore school system. In my student days, the hallways were not patrolled by guards. In fact, they were empty much of the time. You needed a pass to be out during class. Discipline was handled by teachers. Their authority was respected and the students, for the most part, did what they were told. In the old Baltimore, school nurses handed out aspirin and Band-Aids and took care of athletes. In the new Baltimore, the schools have their own police force. Guns and knives are everywhere. Metal detectors line the front doors. Violence is routine. Crack cocaine is king. No one is safe. Students and teachers alike have been assaulted and many feel fear on a daily basis. School nurses give birth-control advice, dress stab wounds and treat kids overdosed on drugs.

Educators, sociologists and politicians disagree about the causes of the precipitous decline of American education. One fact is indisputable: The decline of American education closely parallels the process of secularization in our public schools. This is an uncomfortable fact for many people. It implies that a moral education and decent social behavior are related. The connection between good values and good behavior has long been recognized. The "social contract," the glue that holds society together, has its basis in religion and value-based education. As Jean-Jacques Rousseau argued in 1762, "civil religion" is a social and political necessity. This does not mean that the state should adopt any official religious standard or doctrine. A principal characteristic of civil religion, according to Rousseau, is tolerance of all religious opinions. Further, it assumes that some agreement about moral values is essential to the survival of the republic. And where should those values be taught to successive generations of American citizens? The public schools. Is it just coincidence that the anarchy in our schools has increased dramatically since the removal of prayer in 1963?

Most Americans sense that something important has been lost. Opinion polls show that a majority of American citizens believe their children should have the right to pray in school. A new generation of leaders in the House of Representatives and Senate agrees. Yet for all the sentiment in favor of school prayer, for most citizens the reasons remain heartfelt and intuitive. Most people know something is wrong and believe intuitively that a return to spiritual values is essential to the rehabilitation of American education. This book will give those who are seeking to enter the debate a clearer understanding of the issue. Behind the belief that school prayer is essential to the health of our nation is a historical and philosophical tradition that goes to the very heart of American democracy. As Speaker of the House Newt Gingrich and Congressman Ernest Istook open the national discussion of this issue with the introduction of a new religious freedom amendment to the Constitution, it will be the responsibility of every citizen to make a rational, informed decision. I hope this book will guide you on your way.

# Putting
# Prayer on Trial

The Scottish historian Thomas Carlyle wrote that "history is the essence of innumerable biographies," and his American friend Ralph Waldo Emerson said, "There is properly no history; only biography." Sadly for me, the history of the 1963 school prayer decision is inextricably linked to my personal life and that of my mother, Madalyn Murray O'Hair. My mother, arguably America's most famous atheist, was born on Palm Sunday, 1919, in Beechview, Pennsylvania. Woodrow Wilson was president that year and Prohibition had just been ratified. John Watson published *Psychology from the Standpoint of a Behaviorist,* a radically secular and mechanistic vision of the human psyche. And RCA, a broadcasting company that would chronicle the Supreme Court's school prayer decision forty-four years later, had just been founded. It was an eventful year, and the birth of Madalyn to John and Lena Mays would eventually prove to be noteworthy too. Her turbulent life would affect every schoolchild in America.

My grandparents had ambiguous feelings about religion, but nevertheless had her baptized at a Presbyterian church in Pittsburgh; better safe than sorry. My grandmother, more superstitious than religious, sometimes practiced witchcraft and read tarot cards. Because she was of German ancestry, she taught Mother her first good-night prayer in German. Almost as soon as she could speak, Madalyn began repeating it every night. This was the first and perhaps last prayer she would ever recite. The child's invocation, "I am small, my heart is pure, no one can abide here, but Jesus alone," was my grandmother's idea of cosmic insurance. She was not particularly devoted to Christianity, but had a deep interest in spiritualism and psychic powers. Nightly prayers were part of Mother's early childhood because Grandmother thought them a prudent ritual.

My grandfather was relatively successful as a contractor in the expansionist economy of the 1920s, but went down with the stock market crash in 1929. He would never be prosperous again. In the early days of the Great Depression, he was unable to find work in Pittsburgh and eventually moved the family to a rural Pennsylvania roadhouse. During Prohibition, roadhouses were clandestine taverns and liquor stores, taking advantage of the lax law enforcement outside big cities. His roadhouse was also a part-time brothel. To round out his illegal activities, he ran bootleg liquor up from hillbilly stills in West Virginia. He had his car retrofitted with a custom tank under the backseat and would take little Madalyn with him. My mother's job was to sleep in the back and defer attention from her dad's illegal cargo. These entrepreneurial ventures barely generated enough money to feed the family.

My mother was a complex young woman. Grandfather nicknamed her "the spider" after a pulp-fiction character known for his many alter egos. My mother wore many faces too. In her youth, she exhibited an occasional religious sentiment, once writing in a high school yearbook that she wanted to "serve God for the betterment of man." Whether that desire was from conviction or peer pressure, I do not know. Her behavior always suggested to me a deeply conflicted person. But later in life, she seemed immune to any outside pressure. She would eventually claim to have been an atheist from the age of six. She did not say how a six-year-old arrives at such a serious conclusion. Even a prodigy like Nietzsche was an adult before he decided God was dead. But unlike Nietzsche, Mother never produced an *Ecce Homo* to explain her personal journey to unbelief or, for that matter, any original body of work. Her atheism seemed to grow out of some deeply personal place, an unarticulated anger remarkable in its depth. Mother was never a serious theorist of atheism.

My mother met her first husband, John Roths, in high school. I do not know the story of their romance, but in 1941 they decided to get married and eloped to Cumberland, Maryland. The Day of Infamy, December 7, came two months later. Pearl Harbor marked the entry of the United States into World War II, and both my mother and her husband enlisted. John Roths joined the Marine Corps and was sent to the Pacific theater; my mother joined the Women's Auxiliary Army Corps and sailed to Europe. Mother served in Italy and North Africa as a cryptographer. She was commissioned as a second lieutenant and soon found herself associating with a cadre of urbane, educated men. Her husband, a marine infantryman, quickly faded from memory as she met gentlemen-soldiers from a higher social order. Among them was an 8th Army Air Corps pilot named William J. Murray, Jr. Murray was a New York Brahmin from a large Catholic family. He was married. They had an affair, and I was conceived in September 1945. The same month, Japan officially surrendered on the deck of the USS *Missouri* in Tokyo Harbor. My mother and Murray, however, were not able to reach an accord, and sailed home to separate lives. Later, Mother sued him to establish paternity. She was successful and received fifteen dollars a week for my support.

My mother went to Ohio to seek out her parents to whom she had sent her savings every month during the war. They had moved while she was gone, and when she saw where they lived she was shocked. Home was a dirt-floor shack without running water. Worse, her father had squandered her savings to support his alcoholism. The family was destitute, she was pregnant and her husband—unaware of her infidelity—was due home any day. William J. Murray, Jr., wealthy, religious, socially prominent, would not divorce his wife. He told her bluntly that his religion did not allow it. Living in poverty, barred from a life of comfort and prestige, my mother invested in anger. God became the focus of her hate and the symbol of her abandonment. When John Roths came home and discovered his wife pregnant, he nevertheless decided to stay. In an act of generosity and forgiveness, he offered to be the father of another man's child. Madalyn declined, holding to the hope that somehow Murray would change his mind. She filed for divorce, and by the time I was born on May 25, 1946, it was final. She named me William J. Murray III, and soon after began to call herself Madalyn Murray—even though she had never married my father.

The line between pathos and pathology is hard to draw. My mother's anger at God was remarkable for its intensity. God had "prevented" her from marrying William Murray, Jr. God was the great impediment to her future. In my opinion, this anger propelled her into the school prayer issue with a vengeance—in the truest sense of the word. Mother's anger at God was part of my family's oral tradition before I was born. My grandparents used to tell the story of an incident that happened while Mother was pregnant with me. In the midst of a violent thunderstorm in which a bolt of lightning almost struck our house, she strode into the yard, calling my grandparents to watch. With her audience in place, she challenged God to strike her and her unborn child dead. Nothing happened—for which I am grateful! Although statistical probability was overwhelmingly in her favor, she announced that she had proved "irrefutably" that God did not exist. My mother's forensic shortcomings notwithstanding, her flair for the dramatic was undeniable. This gift would serve her well in the future. Her dramatic confrontation with the Baltimore school district was a masterpiece of high-energy theater.

By 1949, after working various jobs and attending Ashland College, my mother moved the family to Houston, Texas, where she worked as a probation officer for Harris County and attended night classes at the South Texas School of Law. It looked like we might settle in, but in 1952 we moved again—this time to Baltimore, Maryland. Our extended family—mother, son, grandparents and uncle—moved into a small red-brick row house across the street from Northwood Elementary School. It was at Northwood where I remember my first experiences with school prayer. Every morning before starting class, the teacher would repeat a routine that did not seem remarkable at the time. She would read a few verses from a well-worn Bible and lead the class in a recitation of the Lord's Prayer. It never occurred to me to mention this to Mother. In fact, I seldom talked about anything to her. Mother was "Madalyn" to me. My grandparents were my principal caretakers. Her role in my life when I was eight was so poorly defined I did not think of her as a parent.

Soon after this incident, my mother became pregnant again. This time she had no desire to marry the father, who was also married and Catholic, like my father. My half brother was born in November 1954 and named Jon Murray, even though William Murray, Jr., was not his father. My mother had a superstition about illegitimate children. She had heard that they were guaranteed eternal punishment from God unless baptized—an unusual concern for an avowed atheist. Consequently, she had my brother baptized in a Methodist church and even attended services for several months. My mother always had oddly inconsistent feelings about religion. She was not a disinterested atheist. Her attack on school prayer seemed personal, as though directed at a living being. The studied, dispassionate critique of religious belief typical of some intellectuals was not her style. Perhaps her public atheism covered a private struggle against the disquieting temptation to believe. She wasn't angry about God; she was angry *at* God—or so it seemed to me.

From 1952 to 1955, my mother held a succession of jobs including bookkeeper, probation officer, welfare clerk and retail saleswoman. She was never happy and resented the supervision of her managers, all of whom she felt to be incompetent compared to herself. This discontent contributed to her disillusionment with American society and when I was nine, she joined the Socialist Labor party. Before long, the local chapter met next to my bedroom in the basement of our house. I was soon recruited to help this ragtag band of white, disillusioned, middle-class Americans promote their cause. I set up the tables and chairs for meetings, stuffed envelopes and distributed propaganda leaflets. Mother's socialism developed over time into a variant of Soviet-style Marxism. It was rooted in personal grudges against former capitalist employers, anti-Semitism and anger at my grandfather's financial failures. I remember one of her outbursts in which she blamed the country's financial woes on "the Jews in big business." Subsequently, she switched her allegiance to the more radical Socialist Workers party. This was the renegade group founded by Leon Trotsky, the Bolshevik leader who masterminded the November Revolution with Lenin in 1917. Trotsky was expected to succeed Lenin in 1934, but was outmaneuvered by Stalin and eventually murdered in exile. My mother identified with Trotsky and his cause. Later, she would become involved with a pro-Castro group.

Beginning in 1955, my mother subscribed to *USSR,* later renamed *Soviet Life.* A slick, full-color magazine intended to resemble *Life,* it extolled the virtues of Soviet culture. She also subscribed to the *Weekly Worker,* the official organ of the Communist party of the United States, and various other Communist publications. Mother read these journals like travel brochures and decided to move to the Soviet Union. She made her first application for Soviet citizenship and permission to emigrate in 1959 through the embassy in Washington, D.C. She received no response. As the months went by, she continued to send letters and documents to the embassy, including pictures of me and my brother. She claimed at various times to have been an aerospace engineer, attorney, psychiatric social worker and retired field-grade military officer. Embassy officials were unimpressed. By now, I was in junior high at the Woodbourne school. A few months later, she changed strategy and announced that we were traveling to France and reapplying for Soviet citizenship in Paris. For some reason, she thought this would speed the process. We left America on the deck of the old Cunard line's *Queen Elizabeth* on August 24, 1960, bound for Le Havre, France.

In Paris, my mother wasted no time. On a Monday morning we took a cab to the Soviet embassy. The man at the reception desk spoke French but no English. After an agonizing conversation full of pantomime, we understood that we were to return the following day. We did, much to the disappointment of the receptionist. After a week of return visits, someone seemed to understand what we wanted and indicated that it would take some time to make a decision. Weeks later, we were informed by the embassy that the presidium of the Supreme Soviet would have to rule on our request, a process that would take months. The official who delivered this unlikely message took the opportunity to inject a distinct note of pessimism. He said, "I do not believe you have a true comprehension of Marxist principles in our motherland. It is against the law to be unemployed. The punishment for not being employed is hard labor at half pay. In looking at your work record, it seems you would be working for half pay most of the time." Perhaps with visions of rock quarries and sledgehammers in her head, Mother made plans for our immediate return to the United States. Ironically, the lowest fare home was on El Al, the Israeli airline. We boarded an El Al Lockheed Electra at Orly Airport and departed for home, and we landed at Idlewild International Airport. As we approached the customs and immigration booth, my mother began to tremble. As I found out later, she had sent the State Department a letter renouncing her citizenship—and with precise anatomic instructions told them where to put it. The customs agent said, "France on vacation?" My mother froze. I answered for her. "No, sir. Trying to defect." "Very funny," he replied and stamped our passport.

A short time later, my mother reenrolled me at Woodbourne Junior High. Unemployed, she had time to take me to school. Rejected by the Soviets, embarrassed to be back, she was not in a good mood. A few minutes before 8:00 A.M. we pulled up to the redbrick building. The first bell had rung, indicating class would start in five minutes. The sidewalks were clear. We walked up the steps, through the front entrance and into the main hallway. It was deserted. "Why's it so quiet?" she asked. "Everybody's still in homeroom," I replied. We walked down the long hallway, following the signs to the school office. As we passed an open door, my mother noticed students standing, hands over hearts, reciting the Pledge of Allegiance. "They do this every day?" she snorted. As we approached another classroom she stopped dead. The students were standing, heads bowed, reciting the Lord's Prayer. With a burst of obscenities, she shouted, "Why didn't you tell me about this?" "We were going to the Soviet Union to become great commissars," I said with bad timing and complete truthfulness.

In a few moments we were in the counselor's office. Dispensing with the preliminary niceties, Mother got right to the point: "Why are those f---ing children praying? It's un-American and unconstitutional." And in a heated discussion she argued with the counselor for several minutes. Finally she said, "This won't be the last time you hear from me about these prayers in school!" While she was shouting, the counselor filled out an enrollment application, put it into a new manila file folder and marked it with a large *T,* the administrative code for "troublemaker." "If you don't like it, why don't you sue us?" he said. Mother stared at him, registered the idea and left.

On the drive home she began to plan. She instructed me to take notes of what happened during the school day. She wanted records of any activities that hinted of religion in any form: Bible reading, songs, prayers. When I asked why, she replied, "The United States is nothing but a fascist slave-labor camp run by a handful of Jew bankers in New York City. The only way true freedom can be achieved is through the new Socialist man. Only when all men know the truth of their animal sameness will we have true freedom." I knew the speech well. I had heard it many times. Never mind that the connection between "Jew bankers" and Christian prayer seemed rather oblique. This was not logic; it was undifferentiated hate.

The next day I began the log. At Woodbourne Junior High a typical day in my classroom included a student reading two or three Scripture verses, a recital of the Lord's Prayer and the Pledge of Allegiance, which included the phrase "under God." My mother was somewhat disappointed that more egregious examples had not turned up. However, she was undeterred. After two weeks of my undercover work, she sat me down and told me of her intention to demand that the school authorities excuse me from the classroom during the Bible readings, prayers and Pledge of Allegiance, and of her intention to withdraw me from school if they did not comply. The next morning she sent letters outlining her demands to the principal and superintendent of schools. On Wednesday, October 12, Vernon S. Vavrina, the assistant superintendent for secondary schools, telephoned and told my mother the district would not comply with her demands. The next day, I stayed home. Dorothy Duvall, my principal, sent a letter threatening truancy if I did not return. My mother let the situation ride for eight days.

On the ninth day Mother wrote a long letter to the Baltimore *Morning Sun*. She has always had a talent for getting a response out of people, usually by the sheer power of her anger. In her letter, she argued against the custom of public prayer, the phrase "In God we trust" on U.S. coins and the words "under God" in the Pledge of Allegiance. She complained of the "mistreatment of atheists" and argued that the board of education had violated her First and Fourteenth Amendment rights. On that Friday, she drove to the newsstand and picked up a copy of the *Sun*. Nothing. She checked for the next several days, but the letter was not printed.

On Wednesday, October 26, the phone rang. A reporter was on the line. The paper had decided not to print the letter but instead do an interview and print an article–complete with photograph. My mother was ecstatic, but I was not thrilled. I did not want my picture in the paper. I knew there would be a price attached to such publicity; it wasn't the kind of fame I wanted. At four that afternoon a short, soft-spoken reporter rang our doorbell. It was Stephen Nordlinger and a photographer from the *Sun.* My mother invited them in, and we filed through the small living room into the dining room and sat down around the table. Nordlinger took out his notepad and began the interview. "I'm determined that my son is not going to bow down to any concept of what an average American is given to be," my mother said. Making her intentions clear, she emphasized her willingness to take the issue all the way to the Supreme Court. After several minutes, the reporter turned his attention to me.

"Bill, do you mind if I ask you a few questions?" Nordlinger asked. I didn't mind. He went on, "What do you think about your mother taking you out of school?" I gave the answer any normal fourteen-year-old would. He laughed. "But seriously, Bill." Being careful to give the answer my mother wanted, I said, "I think she has done the right thing. As an atheist I shouldn't be subjected to prayer and Bible reading in order to get a free public education." Nordlinger had already interviewed school officials and was aware of my reputation for advocating the Soviet position in class and in my essays. The conversation turned to this topic. My mother's demeanor changed. She did not want her Communist affiliations to muddy the waters. If people

wrote her off as a Communist—and there was good reason to think she was—attention would be diverted from
the issue. Oblivious to this, I prattled on while my
mother sank lower and lower in her chair. The school
officials had accused me of writing an inflammatory,
pro-Soviet paper, among other things. Nordlinger
asked me about it. I volunteered to get it and placed it
on the table in front of him. He scanned the short essay
and said, "Is this all?" It was, I admit, a few words short
of the *Communist Manifesto*. In fact, the paper read like
a vacation brochure for the Communist motherland. At
this point we all stood up, the photographer took a few
pictures and they left.

On Thursday morning, October 27, my young face
appeared on the front page of the *Morning Sun*'s local
news section. The headline read, BOY, 14, BALKS AT
BIBLE READING. The long article covered three
columns. Nordlinger had done a thorough research job.
He noted that this was the first challenge to the school
board rule since its adoption in 1905. The rule required
that the Bible or the Lord's Prayer or both be used in
the opening exercises of all schools under the board's
jurisdiction. He also noted that the board had approved
the Bible for use as a reading book in all schools in
1839, just ten years after the system was founded.

The article also reported that Dr. George B. Brain
was consulting with state educational authorities about
the proper course of action in my case. Brain was holding to a strict, uncompromising line, saying that since
the school district rules made no explicit provision for
those who did not want to participate, I and others like

me must remain in class and be respectful. The article also reported my mother's discomfort with a textbook, *The Story of the Nations,* in my world history class. According to my mother, I had objected to a reproduction of Da Vinci's *Last Supper* in the book (I hadn't). My mother was quoted as saying that the textbook issue was secondary and negotiable but the matter of the opening exercises was not. The article concluded with a reprinting of my entire report on the Soviet Union.

We ceased to be private citizens that morning. Before I finished reading the article, the phone started to ring. A frenzy of reporters were eager to cover this unusual human interest story. Baltimore was a religious city in those days, predominately Catholic, and our antireligious crusade was an instant controversy. The local affiliates of NBC, CBS and ABC called to arrange on-camera interviews. A journalist from Washington telephoned, as did a network news team from New York. Reporters from the wire services showed up at our front door. As soon as my mother would hang up the phone, it would ring again. G. K. Chesterton has said, "Journalism largely consists of saying 'Lord Jones is dead' to people who never knew Lord Jones was alive." On Wednesday school prayer was a nonissue in the popular media; by Friday, it was national news. That evening I watched myself on television. It was intoxicating. Mother kept flipping between stations, trying to take it all in. At her direction, I took photos of the screen with my 35-mm camera (the VCR had not yet been invented).

In the midst of Thursday's media inquiries, Fred Weisgal from the American Civil Liberties Union called. He told my mother that the organization was entering the case on my behalf and advised her to send me back to school. If the issue was prayer, my truancy only confused matters. The point was to force a legal confrontation. If the school expelled me solely for refusing to stay in class during the Bible reading and prayer, then the issue would be clearly defined in any impending litigation. My mother was delighted to have the ACLU's help. Exercising her natural gift for political theater, she telephoned the networks and told them I would be returning to school the next day. Could they send camera crews to cover the event? The editors sensed the potential of the story and agreed to be at our house early the next morning.

At 6:30 A.M. I awoke, dressed and ate breakfast. I planned to walk to school, as I usually did. The reporters and camera crews showed up on cue. Mother immediately engaged them in a strategy session. She wanted to give them the most compelling footage possible. It was agreed that everyone would follow me at a distance in cars, cameras rolling. That would give any "Christians" along the route who wanted to throw rocks or punches the opportunity to do so without feeling intimidated. "We certainly wouldn't want to intimidate any thugs," I thought to myself. One reporter asked Mother what hospital I would be taken to if I was injured. Journalism as blood sport. The walk to school was beginning to seem like a gauntlet. Would the sidewalk be lined with jeering crowds? Fear rose in me.

I stepped out the door at 7:15, under the curious gaze of a dozen neighbors. I felt excited and sick at the same time. It was a two-mile walk to school. The sidewalk on my street was empty. Thank God. Or thank something. The morning was brisk with a few clouds floating in the sky; the trees were dressed in autumn leaves. I had missed eleven days of school since our return from France. The pace of events had been dizzying. The morning newspaper was already on the streets and the headline read BOY TO SEEK TO RETURN TO SCHOOL TODAY. The subhead read, "[Superintendent] Brain Says He Will Be Suspended If He Avoids Exercises." The folded newspapers on every stoop reminded me of my lost anonymity. My mother had, of course, called Stephen Nordlinger at the *Sun* and explained her strategy, including the advice of the ACLU. Consequently, the article both anticipated a dramatic showdown and created the conditions necessary for it to happen. My mother's instructions to me were to withdraw conspicuously and avoid participation in the prayer. According to the newspaper, this would guarantee my expulsion. I mused on these things as I walked. Occasionally I looked over my shoulder to check on the camera crews. They were creeping along in cars about a block behind. Two reporters walked together on the sidewalk near the cars.

About half an hour into my walk I began to notice other Woodbourne students on their way to school. No one seemed to recognize me. I was relieved. In another few minutes, I was within blocks of the school. Then it began. A loud voice from behind me said,

"Why don't you move to Russia?" I thought to myself, "We tried." Another voice soon rang out, "Commie lover!" I could hear other kids laugh. The closer I got to school the more catcalls came my way. Few taunts, if any, were aimed at my atheism. The possibility that I was a Communist seemed to be the most troubling to my tormentors. I was embarrassed and angry, but no one attacked me or threw anything. The news crews were undoubtedly disappointed.

By 8:00 A.M., I reached the steps of the school. As students streamed through the doors, several teachers stood guard. Their assignment was to prevent the press from entering the building—*and* find me. As I stepped into the foyer, a teacher stopped me and pointed to the administrative offices. "Why?" I asked. "You're to see Dr. Vavrina," he replied. I didn't want to go. Why would an important guy from downtown want to see me? I decided to go to my homeroom first so I wouldn't be counted absent. This was not what the teacher wanted, but he did not prevent me. I ran down the now-empty hall. When I reached my homeroom, the door was locked. I could see the principal, Miss Duvall, through the small window speaking earnestly to the students. They could see me, but wouldn't let me in. Having no choice, I reluctantly walked down the hall to the school office.

Inside the principal's office sat Vernon Vavrina. The man with the alliterative name looked pained. He was as uncomfortable to be there as I was. He introduced himself. "I usually work downtown, Bill, but I came here today to see if I could help things go a little more smoothly." I grunted an acknowledgment. He asked me to sit down. "I understand that you have some objection to our opening exercises. Is that true?" I answered in the affirmative. He asked me several questions about my religious background. I told him I just wanted to be left alone and go to school. After a few more questions, the interview ended. He told me to report to the school office every morning before first period, rather than go to my homeroom. I returned to class and was met by an embarrassed silence. Everyone ignored me—until I arrived at the playing field. On that day, and for several days thereafter, I was the victim of beatings. Kids would find opportunity to assault me, leaving hurriedly to avoid unwanted attention. No one was ever caught. My bruises recorded the daily attacks. They were the stigmata of the post-McCarthy era. "Commie" was the usual epithet. We lived in an ethnic working-class neighborhood. Many of our neighbors were Polish and Hungarian Catholics who had escaped the violence of Communist countries. Our family wanted to replace the democracy they had sought in America with the same godless totalitarianism that they had escaped from. Some had lost loved ones to Communist gulags. In my eagerness to please my mother and her Marxist friends, I was ignorant of the pain I caused my neighbors.

C. Ferdinand Sybert, the attorney general of Maryland, at the request of the school district, ruled on our complaint on Thursday, November 3, 1960. In his decision, he stated that reading the Bible in school was constitutional and that anyone who absented himself from school to avoid this practice could be prosecuted for truancy. He recommended that those who objected to it be allowed to remain silent or be excused from the opening exercises. This was a small victory. We had won the right to be excused. It seemed like a reasonable decision to me. The majority of students could pray while I could opt out. It wasn't a moral victory for me; I was too young for that and I didn't have a real ideology yet. As far as I was concerned, I had just won the right to read science-fiction books in the hall.

But Mother was not about to quit and claim victory. The process had taken on a life of its own. She was an instant celebrity. The media loved her coarse, confrontational style. Reporters were learning new Anglo-Saxon words. Mother could smoke, drink and cuss like the boys. The reporters liked to hang out with her. She was the perfect media maven. *And* she was making money. The mail at 1561 Winford Road had increased tenfold. Every aging Trotskyite, social anarchist and antireligious misfit in the country was sending cash. Carl Brown, a self-styled atheist and nudist, sent five thousand dollars. He later gave my mother 160 acres of land to found an atheist/nudist university. The gifts kept coming, tens of thousands of dollars. It was too good to be true.

And we were receiving pro bono legal assistance. The ACLU had pulled out of the case, but a local attorney named Leonard Kerpelman had telephoned and offered to help. At first Mother put him off, unsure of his credentials. Instead, she turned to Harold Buchman, an attorney she said had represented the Communist party in Maryland. Hedging her bet, she took Kerpelman with her to the first meeting with Buchman. Buchman signed on, and his name appeared along with Kerpelman's on the legal papers filed in the superior court of Baltimore. But soon after the petition was filed, Buchman dropped out and by default Leonard Kerpelman became the attorney of record. It was he who would eventually guide the case all the way to the Supreme Court.

Madalyn Murray and Leonard Kerpelman were an odd couple. In spite of the anti-Semitic slurs my mother had uttered dozens of times in my presence, she accepted this legal marriage of convenience with Mr. Kerpelman, an Orthodox Jew. She was pleased that he allowed her to do much of the work, thus putting into practice what she had learned at the South Texas School of Law. She was unable to act as her own attorney because she had failed the bar exam three times. She did, however, write and direct most of the legal work on the case. It is pure irony that the arguments for one of the most important issues ever to reach the Supreme Court were written by someone who had failed the bar. While Leonard and Madalyn worked on the legal battle, I fought my own skirmishes on the schoolyard and in the neighborhood. Squads of Commie beaters terrorized me on a regular basis.

On December 7, 1960—Pearl Harbor Day—our attorney filed a petition for a writ of mandamus with the superior court of Baltimore that asked the court to issue an order stopping the "illegal" Bible reading and prayer exercises. It stated that my religious liberty had been impinged by giving preference to religious belief over unbelief. It went on to say that even when allowed to leave the classroom during these "offensive" proceedings, I was losing "caste" with my peers and "being subjected to reproach and insult." In mid-January 1961, the school board filed a brief of demurrer, which argued that the facts as we had presented them were true but were not worthy of the court's attention.

On March 2, Judge J. Gilbert Pendergast heard our case. On April 27, he dismissed our petition. In his memorandum he said, "It is abundantly clear that petitioners' real objective is to drive every concept of religion out of the public school system.... Thus the beliefs of virtually all the pupils would be subordinated to those of Madalyn Murray and her son. Any reference to the Declaration of Independence would be prohibited because it concludes with the historic words of the signers ... 'with a firm reliance on the protection of Divine Providence.'..." The next day Mother and Kerpelman filed a petition with the Maryland Court of Appeals. Nearly a year after the faulted defection to the Soviet Union and in the midst of this case she still held out hope for Soviet citizenship. It was April 1961, and Soviet cosmonaut Yuri Gagarin had just become the first man in space. Despite my mother's financial success with the prayer case, she decided to endear herself to the Soviet embassy by having me clip every reference to Gagarin I could find and glue them into a scrapbook. I clipped and glued for weeks. Ultimately, my mother drove me to Washington and deposited me at the front door of the Soviet embassy. I handed the scrapbook to some minor official. Nothing ever came of it.

The court of appeals heard the petition the next month. My mother took me out of school and we drove together to Annapolis to watch Kerpelman present the case. According to Mother, it did not go well. She was furious with Kerpelman, but she could not get rid of him. No one else was willing to take the case for free. Kerpelman was working for court costs only. Soon after the initial hearing, the appeals court sent word that the entire seven-judge panel wanted to rehear the constitutional arguments. Kerpelman appeared again. After that, it was a waiting game. Three months later, on April 6, 1962, the court ruled 4 to 3 against us. The majority opinion stated that "neither the First nor the Fourteenth Amendment was intended to stifle all rapport between religion and government." There was only one place to go. On May 15, Kerpelman appealed the case to the United States Supreme Court.

In the meantime, Mother was putting her newfound funds to good use. She invested three thousand dollars in the purchase of a new A. B. Dick printing press and on July 1, 1962 published the first issue of the *American Atheist.* We installed the press in our basement where the local chapter of the Socialist Workers party used to meet. We soon had a complete print shop. Mother made good money on subscriptions, which helped her promote our court case—and in turn raise more funds through donations. About this time, the Communist party also helped out financially by putting Mother in charge of what amounted to a franchise for their third bookstore in America. The store was called the New Era Book Shop, and it was located on 22nd Street in downtown Baltimore. The store was heavily subsidized by the Soviets, who supplied the wholesale stock at greatly reduced prices, including full-color art books for pennies.

Throughout the remainder of 1962, preparatory work continued for the upcoming court case. But aside from my mother's self-promotion through the *American Atheist,* the issue enjoyed little publicity. Other events had taken over the headlines. The Soviets had begun to arm Cuba and President Kennedy had ordered the Cuban blockade. The U-2 spy plane pilot Francis Gary Powers was released by the Soviets after a complex negotiation process. The Telstar satellite was launched, and Americans worried about falling behind in the "space race." American astronauts John Glenn and Scott Carpenter orbited the Earth. The civil rights movement was grabbing headlines as federal troops were sent to the University of Mississippi to ensure the admission of its first black applicant, James Meredith. John Steinbeck and Linus Pauling received Nobel Prizes for literature and peace. Moviegoers were flocking to see *The Manchurian Candidate* and *Lawrence of Arabia.* Who cared about the school prayer issue? Except for my mother, not many.

On Tuesday, February 26, 1963, the Supreme Court began its hearing on our case. The alarm went off early that morning. I got up and sleepily put on my best clothes. When I came upstairs, Mother was already dressed to kill in a white imitation-fur coat with matching hat and gloves. This was very unusual. Mother was not unfashionable in the usual sense. She was antifashion. She took pleasure in shunning "bourgeois taste," never wore makeup and practiced a kind of studied dishevelment. But this morning she was the very picture of middle-class sartorial splendor. I looked like a teenager in a scaled-down ill-fitting adult business suit. I tugged at my tie as we got into our huge Oldsmobile 88 for the drive to Washington. We picked up Leonard Kerpelman and his wife and carpooled the fifty miles into the heart of the capital city. Mother talked excitedly the whole way. William J. Murray III, Plaintiff, slumped in the backseat, wishing the whole dreary episode was over.

We parked near the courthouse and walked around the block to the entrance. The white marble edifice gleamed in the morning sun. As we mounted the steps, the Capitol dome was behind us; history surrounded us. I read the inscription on the pediment above the Greek columns: EQUAL JUSTICE UNDER THE LAW. It was like entering a cathedral. The architecture of the place made you feel small and insignificant. We walked through the massive brass doors with their bas-relief figures and made our way down a grand marble-lined hall that led straight into the courtroom. The iconography of power was everywhere. I was impressed.

At 9:30 A.M., the justices, clad in judicial vestments, entered the room. The gallery was full and many reporters were present. Everyone stood as a clerk called in a loud voice, "Oyez, oyez. God save the United

States and this honorable Court!" My mother groaned and shook her head. We sat down at the appropriate time and my eyes scanned the dais in front of me. To my discomfort, I found several pairs of judicial eyes squarely focused on me. We were in the front row, and I was under the panoptic gaze of nine somber justices. I squirmed in my seat while trying to look as serious and dignified as I could.

After a few preliminary formalities, Leonard Kerpelman rose and with unsure legs wobbled to the podium. He cleared his throat nervously and began his presentation. He said that prayer in public schools had been tolerated for so long that it had become traditional and that anything that is unconstitutional does not become constitutional through tradition. He told the Court that the Constitution had erected a "wall of separation" between church and state. Justice Potter Stewart interrupted, asking where this wording appears in the text. Stewart knew that it did not. Kerpelman was stumped and an embarrassing silence ensued. When he regained his composure, he said that the text was not explicit on this point but had been interpreted to mean that.

This contention opened up a brief free-for-all with the judges asking questions of all the attorneys and of each other. The meaning of the "free exercise clause" of the First Amendment was also debated at length. My attention faded as the arguments continued throughout the day. After adjournment, we commuted home and my mother prepared to return the next day. Teenagers have no sense of history. I decided to return to school and skip the remaining proceedings. With the close of Court Wednesday, the hearing was over. Now it was time to wait.

As the justices began to deliberate the issue unusual alliances formed. The National Council of Churches and several Jewish organizations weighed in on our side. The attorneys general of eighteen states filed amicus curiae briefs in support of the defendants. Not a single Christian organization filed a brief in support of school prayer. In March, *Life* magazine ran an editorial arguing that the nation's founders had wanted the "leaven" of religion in public life and spoke in favor of school prayer. The title of the article was "The Bible: Better in School Than in Court." Mother wrote a letter in response.

> ...The atheist's position is one arrived at after considerable study, cogitation and inner search. It is a position which is founded in science, in reason and in a love for fellow man rather than in a love for God.
>
> We find the Bible to be nauseating, historically inaccurate, replete with the ravings of madmen. We find God to be sadistic, brutal, and a representation of hatred, vengeance. We find the Lord's Prayer to be that muttered by worms groveling for meager existence in a traumatic, paranoid world.
>
> This is not appropriate untouchable dicta to be forced on adult or child. The business of the public schools, where attendance is compulsory, is to prepare children to face the problems on earth, not to prepare for heaven, which is a delusional dream of the unsophisticated minds of the ill-educated clergy....

Mother was not intellectually sophisticated or particularly well educated herself, but she certainly knew how to inflame passions. At that she was a genius. Her blunt rhetoric offended even those who agreed with her on the school prayer issue. The intellectual left would have nothing to do with her. The religious groups that supported her position kept a wary distance. So this odd consortium of atheists, Christians and Jews awaited the decision.

On June 17, 1963, the Court finally rendered its opinion. Supreme Court decisions are presented quietly, in writing. A clerk stacks copies of the printed-and-bound decision like so many tabloids at a newsstand. No one reads it aloud. You have to read it yourself. There is no courtroom ceremony, no legal pageantry to mark the occasion. And so by means of this prosaic and bureaucratic gesture the momentous decision was handed down.

# A Benevolent
# Neutrality?

By an overwhelming vote of 8 to 1, the Supreme Court
reversed the Maryland Court of Appeals decision and
ruled that Bible reading and prayer exercises were
unconstitutional. The decision made the front page of
newspapers across the country. *The New York Times*
headline read SUPREME COURT, 8 TO 1, PROHIBITS
LORD'S PRAYER AND BIBLE READING AS PUBLIC SCHOOL
REQUIREMENTS. Press accounts told how mainstream
Protestants and Jews favored the decision while Roman
Catholics, evangelicals and fundamentalists opposed it.
Billy Graham said that he was "shocked at the decision." Harry Truman, the plainspoken former president, said prayer "never hurt anybody" and made
"good citizens out of them." A follow-up story in *The
New York Times* told how the decision would affect 41
percent of the nation's school districts in thirty-seven

states. At the time of the decision, only eleven states did not permit Bible readings. *Newsweek* reported that a Chicago high school had responded to the decision by removing a praying mantis from its biology collection. At least some people had a sense of humor about it. My mother's chance encounter at Woodbourne Junior High changed school practices all over America.

This is the law the Court struck down:

> Each school, either collectively or in classes, shall be opened by the reading, without comment, of a chapter in the Holy Bible [the King James Version] and/or the use of the Lord's Prayer. The Douay [Roman Catholic version] may be used by those pupils who prefer it. Appropriate patriotic exercises should be held as a part of the general opening exercise of the school or class. Any child shall be excused from participating in the opening exercises or from attending the opening exercises upon written request of his parent or guardian.

The opinion of the Court was written by Justice Tom C. Clark and concurred in by all the other members of the Court except Justice Stewart. It is true, said Justice Clark, that religion has been closely identified with our history and government. The fact that the founding fathers believed devotedly that there is a God and that the inalienable rights of man are rooted in Him is clearly evidenced in their writings, from the Mayflower Compact to the Constitution. Today, he said, our oaths of office, from the president's to an alderman's, end with the supplication "So help me God" (which, of course, my mother strenuously objected to). Congress, he noted, opens with a prayer, and the crier of the

Supreme Court invokes the grace of God in declaring the sessions of the Court open.

However, Clark continued, it is equally true that religious freedom is embedded in our public and private life. Freedom to worship is indispensable in a country whose people come from the "four quarters of the earth" and have brought with them a diversity of religious opinions. Under this ideal of religious freedom it has long been recognized that government must be *neutral and, while protecting all, must prefer none and disparage none.* Examining earlier decisions that interpreted the words "Congress shall make no law respecting an establishment of religion or prohibiting the free exercise thereof," Clark stated that the Court had repeatedly held that the ban on establishment is applicable to the states, just as it is to the federal government. Clark reaffirmed the Court's earlier rejection of the contention that the establishment clause forbids only governmental preference of one religion over another. "Neither a state nor the Federal Government can set up a church. Neither can pass laws which aid one religion, aid all religions, or prefer one religion over another." Clark dismissed the arguments of those who questioned its handling of history and logic, saying their arguments were "entirely untenable and of value only as academic exercises." Continuing, he said:

> . . . The Establishment Clause has been directly considered by this Court eight times in the past score of years and, with only one Justice dissenting on the point it has consistently held that the clause withdrew all legislative power respecting religious belief or the

expression thereof. The test may be stated as follows: what are the purpose and the primary effect of the enactment? If either is the advancement or inhibition of religion then the enactment exceeds the scope of legislative power as circumscribed by the Constitution. That is to say that to withstand the strictures of the Establishment Clause *there must be a secular legislative purpose* [emphasis added] and a primary effect that neither advances nor inhibits religion.... The Free Exercise Clause, likewise considered many times here, withdraws from legislative power, state and Federal, the exertion of any restraint on the free exercise of religion. Its purpose is to secure religious liberty in the individual by prohibiting any invasions thereof by civil authority. Hence it is necessary in a free exercise case for one to show the coercive effect of the enactment as it operates against him in the practice of his religion. The distinction between the two clauses is apparent–a violation of the Free Exercise Clause is predicated on coercion while the Establishment Clause violation need not be so attended.

Applying these principles to my case, the Court found that the prayer and Bible reading statute was of a religious nature, and therefore unconstitutional. Religious exercises that are "required by law as part of a school's curriculum" violate the First Amendment's ban on laws respecting an establishment of religion. The school authorities had argued that the purpose of the morning prayer and Bible reading was not religious but secular. They asserted that the statute sought to "promote moral values, contradict the materialistic trends of the time, perpetuate democracy and teach literature," and, they

added, it was "optional." Justice Clark disagreed and
responded by saying that the "invalidity" of these practices was not "mitigated" by the fact that it was
optional (the right to be excused was a victory my
mother had won in the lower courts). Nor is it a
defense, Clark argued, that the religious practices were
relatively minor violations of the First Amendment.
"The breach of neutrality that is today a trickling stream
may all too soon become a raging torrent and, in the
words of Madison, 'it is proper to take alarm at the first
experiment on our liberties.'" Clark claimed that the
banning of religious exercises did not establish a "religion of secularism" or exhibit any hostility to religion.
The "religious exercises, required by the Baltimore
School District were in violation of the 'command of
the First Amendment that the Government maintain
strict neutrality, neither aiding nor opposing religion.'"
The opinion concluded with this statement:

> The place of religion in our society is an exalted one,
> achieved through a long tradition of reliance on the
> home, the church and the inviolable citadel of the
> individual heart and mind. We have come to recog-
> nize through bitter experience that it is not within the
> power of government to invade that citadel, whether
> its purpose or effect be to aid or oppose, to advance
> or retard. In the relationship between man and reli-
> gion, the State is firmly committed to a position of
> neutrality.

As we view this case in the light of a new day the question for us to consider—or reconsider—is why this decision was made and how the justices argued in support
of it. The principles upon which the decision was made

have established a legal precedent that remains in force to this day. The Supreme Court, of course, does not work in isolation. It establishes principles that are used by the lower courts and influences policies instituted by state agencies, local school districts, principals and teachers. Only the Supreme Court itself can rescind or change its decisions. It is the penultimate authority in these matters. The people, through their elected officials, are the ultimate authority. And perhaps the people will exercise their authority through the passage of a new constitutional amendment. But if we do so, we must understand the issues at stake. This makes an examination of the Court's decision exceedingly important. We must know where the Court has gone wrong before we can make it right. Fortunately, our open democratic system of government makes this possible. The Supreme Court's decisions are not shrouded in secrecy. The justices publish them in lengthy, carefully worded documents. Each justice must declare his or her assent or dissent. Consequently, Court records preserve a fascinating glimpse of judicial wisdom and folly, consensus and division, continuity and change.

In deciding my case, the justices published a document 183 pages long. It contained the decision itself, relevant case law, the majority opinion, assenting opinions and a lone dissent. The justices' supporting arguments form the bulk of the document and are interesting in a number of respects. As we would expect, they are historically conditioned and informed by the beliefs, backgrounds and basic assumptions of the justices themselves. The Court's decision went far beyond matters of legal technicality. The justices employed reasoning that required the use of history, textual criticism, philosophy and social theory. The Court is a maker of social policy. It would be naïve to think of the school prayer decision simply in legal terms, requiring only legal judgment. The Supreme Court is a high calling, requiring broad wisdom, in-depth knowledge, excellent critical faculties and an open mind. The Court's decisions affect many important aspects of our day-to-day life and, consequently, Court opinions should be the concern of every citizen. The insular quality of the Court does not extend to its decisions. When published, they enter the marketplace of ideas and become the nation's community property. It is the responsibility of an involved, democratic citizenry to examine and test those decisions.

As a child, I supported the Court's decision. As an adult, I have come to see it as critically flawed, and I regret my role as the plaintiff. In my opinion, the wheels my mother and I set in motion have done great harm to education in this nation. But we were only partially responsible for the result. The Court had been actively redefining social policy for more than three decades when our case came before it. The Warren Court was only continuing a process of secularization begun much earlier. Our case was one more nail in the coffin. Religious education had already been declared dead by the Court.

Over a period of years, the Court defined and implemented a policy of secularization that was deliberate and calculated. In deciding which cases to hear, the Court sought out those that gave it the opportunity to fashion a rigid doctrine of secularism which was inherently hostile to religion. In the process, the justices utilized a rationale based on an interpretation of history that has been widely criticized. In all of their decisions regarding religion and education, the justices based their findings on the writings and actions of our nation's founders. They invoked the icons of a great tradition: Thomas Jefferson, James Madison, Roger Williams and John Locke. Of course, they were right to do this but, in my opinion, they got it wrong on many key points.

The history of how we achieved religious freedom in this country is colorful and fascinating–a story full of intrigue. But it does not lend support to the radical separation of church and state that resulted from the justices' decision. As we unpack this history later, we will look at many of the people, places and events to which the justices referred. I think the historical evidence suggests that the Warren Court skewed that history in support of a decision fundamentally at odds with it. As we examine the history to which they refer, we must keep in mind several key questions. How did our religious freedoms come to be institutionalized in the Constitution? What exactly did the founders intend to protect with the First Amendment? What did church-state separation mean to them? What did Thomas Jefferson think about the role of religion in public education? What about James Madison? The Court itself has raised these questions. The answers are of concern to us all.

**secularization** (sec´u•lar•i•za´tion), *n.* 1. the social or
political process of rejecting all forms of religious
faith. 2. the elimination of any religious element within public education and other civic institutions.

The one thread that runs through the entire decision is
that of secularism. I mentioned in the introduction that
this theme is integral to the school prayer controversy.
The justices were very explicit in their commitment to
secular education but what does this mean? For the justices, secularism was synonymous with neutrality. They
stated very forcefully that a secular education was, in
their opinion, demanded by the First Amendment. For
them, the alternative to the establishment of religion
was the endorsement of a purely secular neutrality. In
this respect, they were completely consistent with the
prevailing ideology among social scientists and educational theorists of their time. The zeitgeist of the 1960s,
among most intellectuals, was decidedly secular.
Consistent with that spirit was the notion that secular
education was value free. This idea, in turn, was a
reflection of the prevailing arrogance of many social
scientists who believed their disciplines were above
matters of morality or subjectivity. This arrogance even
has a name.

In the 1960s many social scientists embraced a doctrine known by the German philosophical term
*Wertfreiheit,* which means "value free." According to this
doctrine scientific opinions (including opinions in the
social sciences like education) were free of ideological
bias and ethically neutral. A good example of this can
be found in a standard reference work from the period,

the 1967 edition of the *Encyclopedia of Philosophy.* This work, a compendium of articles written by mainstream scholars, was openly disdainful of critics (and there were not very many) who suggested that the social sciences might be value laden. In fact, this idea seemed so preposterous to one author that he felt it hardly worth his effort to refute.

There were, however, a few eloquent critics of secular neutrality–especially among religious scholars and sociologists. Talcott Parsons, a sociologist at Harvard, asserted that no society or knowledge system could possibly exist apart from values and biases. But Parsons's view was not widely known, or shared, by many of his colleagues. A religious scholar, Mary Harkness, published a book in 1952 entitled *The Modern Rival of Christian Faith: An Analysis of Secularism.* Harkness labeled one kind of secularism "scientism," a belief system she considered to be in competition with religion. She wrote: "A new form of 'comparative religion' has emerged … [among these religions] are scientism, humanism, democracy, nationalism, racism, and fascism, capitalism, and communism … each in some way is an active rival … [each is] a religion … each in its own way provides a faith, a hope, and a love. [Each] calls forth a devotion beyond itself.…"

A few secular humanists acknowledged the religious nature of their "faith." A year after the Court's decision an article appeared in *Humanist Magazine* entitled "What's Wrong with Humanism." The article proposed the formation of a commission to develop a humanist "bible," hymns and liturgy. But not many people read

*Humanist Magazine,* and the great majority of intellectuals and policy makers believed in secular neutrality without question. Harkness said, "[Secularism] seldom comes labeled, and most of its exponents, if questioned, would say that they are simply truth seekers who believe in intelligence and good will. Its presence, however, is all around us...."

Since the 1960s, the nature of secularism has engaged the interest of people across the political/ideological spectrum. The Court today exists in a different intellectual climate. There are still proponents of the idea that secularism is value free but these people are now intellectual anachronisms. The attack on secularism has come from both the left and the right. The destruction of the value-free myth has created strange intellectual bedfellows. Certainly, the critics of secularism have widely divergent goals, methods, political philosophies and attitudes about religion, but they have one thing in common: the belief that secularism is infused with values.

Among conservative Christians, the term "secular humanism" is frequently used as a cipher for a whole complex of issues relating to social values and the process of secularization. There is a significant body of literature going back many years in which this issue has been raised and discussed in books intended for popular audiences. Among the best known popularizers of the issue was Francis Schaeffer, a conservative evangelical writer. Schaeffer wrote extensively about the decline of Western civilization and the rise of secularism. His best-selling books were read by a wide audience of college students and young adults in the 1970s. His son, Franky, wrote a sharp critique of secularism in 1982 entitled *A Time for Anger: The Myth of Neutrality*. According to Franky Schaeffer, "In the guise of advocating 'neutrality,' secular humanists have replaced our nation's set of operating principles ... and have effectively established secular humanism as the only national religion." Many other conservative writers, running the gamut from fundamentalist preachers to mainstream politicians, have contributed to the discussion. William Bennett in his 1992 book, *The De-Valuing of America,* said, "Neutrality to religion turns out to bring with it neutrality to those values that issue from religion. The new source of divisiveness is the assault of secularism on religion."

The left has produced penetrating critiques of secularism as well. Numerous scholars from the loosely defined postmodernist movement have written extensively on the issue. Historians and social philosophers like the late French scholar Michel Foucault have published brilliant accounts of the demise of the sacred and the rise of secularism. Works like Foucault's *The Order of Things: An Archaeologie of Human Sciences,* first published in 1966, examined the development of contemporary secular thought in exhaustive detail.

A major theme of contemporary academia is the "fiction" of value-free neutrality. Unknown to the justices was the rising tide of scholarship that was undermining their ideology. That tide is now a flood, and a trip to any university library will provide ample evidence of the change. There you will find hundreds, if not thousands, of books and journal articles discussing the impossibility of value-free *anything.* As it turns out, the intellectual currents have been slowly changing direction since the turn of the century. The whole notion of value-free secular knowledge is under vigorous attack from all sides and in all academic disciplines. Can any educational system be free of bias? These days, a thousand scholars are ready to argue no. A scan of the card catalog reveals that the attack is rooted in the works of famous thinkers we would not readily associate with this issue.

One of them is everyone's favorite genius, Albert Einstein. To the average American, Einstein was a brilliant physicist. To the academic, he was the guy who forever muddied the waters of value-free objectivity. Einstein's work suggests that no person is a neutral observer because everything is relative. According to Einstein's interpreters, this is not to say there are no rules. They make a subtle point: A person never stands apart from any process or idea, no matter whether that person is a scientist trying to "capture" a subatomic particle or an educational theorist trying to develop a value-free curriculum. Every system brings with it a set of assumptions and values.

Another famous thinker whose work has contributed to the demise of value-free ideology is Sigmund Freud. Freud's interpreters have pointed out that one implication of his work (regarding the subconscious) is the impossibility of being consistently objective in our day-to-day lives. They conclude from this that values and biases affect every person and every intellectual pursuit. Even when we are not aware of it, our values are betrayed in more ways than we intend and our actions often mean more than we may say. These are just two examples of many influential thinkers whose works are being examined by contemporary scholarship in the context of social values. More and more, the hubris of late nineteenth- and early twentieth-century secularism is being challenged.

The new avant-garde believes that secular assumptions have been "constructed" by social processes involving the exercise of power, not some dispassionate, scientific discovery of objective, neutral values. They argue that it is in the nature of secular values to conceal themselves in the unspoken and unconscious decisions of institutional powers (Freud). In other words, secularism gained credibility only as it became empowered by school curricula, court decisions and state policies, many of which have been unconsciously motivated (Foucault). The notion of value-free secularism is, therefore, only a useful fiction, greasing the wheels of social life.

The avant-garde has come to believe that everything in life, from the most fundamental elements of matter (Einstein) to the most profound aspects of the human mind, are influenced and/or perceived on the basis of values. These are the ideas that are flourishing with a new generation of intellectual leaders. It has made for an uneasy and interesting marriage of the right and the left. Liberal scholars and conservative Christians both agree on the impossibility of value-free neutrality while disagreeing on just about everything else. It is time to renegotiate the meaning of secular neutrality. Perhaps the best we can do is establish a level playing field for every viewpoint, from the sacred to the secular. But to do so, we must dispose of, now and forever, the myth that secularism is not a competing ideology.

Given the spirit of the time in which the Warren Court grew up, it is hardly surprising that it exhibited the intellectual biases it did. Five members of the 1963 Court—more than half—were born before the turn of the century. Hugo Black, the oldest, was born in 1886 and Byron White, the youngest, in 1917. Five of the justices graduated from college before 1922. All of these men were educated in a period in which science was ascendant and secularism was its new religion. The "demythologizing" of the world through scientific and secular means was moving ahead at full speed.

John Watson, a professor at Johns Hopkins from 1908 to 1920, was typical of the attitudes to be found on the campuses of that era: "[Psychology and the social sciences are] a purely objective, experimental branch of natural science." Humans were well on their way to being transformed into "independent variables," objectified and classified subjects of secular inquiry. University education, particularly in prestigious schools, was in the romantic embrace of leading secular intellectuals like Bertrand Russell. Russell taught on and off from 1895 until the 1960s at Cambridge. He wrote a famous book, *Why I Am Not a Christian,* in 1957. Philosophers like Hegel and Nietzsche (and many others including Marx) were among the intellectual obsessions of academics. Hegel was studied for his assertion that the human mind had progressed from "mere consciousness" to "absolute knowledge." By that he meant "objective," secular knowledge. Nietzsche was studied for his vehement repudiation of Christian ethics and all things religious.

It would be unfair to suggest that the justices were entirely shaped by these influences. The point is this: It would have been impossible for them *not* to have been influenced to *some* degree. This was the intellectual milieu of their time. Faith in secularism was at an all-time high. The relationship between religion and secularism was being redefined. The façades of new university buildings no longer bore the inscriptions of saints. They were more likely to give tribute to secular objectivity. When it came time to build a social science building, the University of Chicago put this inscription over the door: "When you cannot express it in numbers, your knowledge is of a meager and unsatisfactory kind." Unfortunately, decades of quantitative studies in educational theory have not produced an improvement in moral values.

What the Supreme Court did not recognize was the extent to which secularism had become dogma and was, in fact, a value system in competition with religion. The school prayer case was not fundamentally partisan. Four of the nine justices were appointed by Republican President Dwight D. Eisenhower. Clark (Truman), who wrote the majority decision, was joined by Earl Warren (Eisenhower), Hugo Black (Roosevelt) and Byron White (Kennedy). The majority decision represented a cross section of political viewpoints. The unifying factor was not party allegiance but a belief in secular neutrality.

The Court's task, however, was not to define secular neutrality but to decide if and how the First Amendment applied to school prayer. The first lines of the First Amendment read "Congress shall make no law respecting an establishment of religion, or prohibiting the free exercise thereof;..." These two clauses are called the establishment clause and the free exercise clause and to which the justices made repeated reference. The justices also referred to the Fourteenth Amendment, into which the First Amendment is absorbed.

This amendment guarantees all citizens of the United States ". . . nor shall any State deprive any person of life, liberty, or property, without due process of law; nor deny to any person within its jurisdiction the equal protection of the laws." The Court, based on a landmark 1940 decision, took this to mean that the First Amendment applied to the states as well as to the federal government. The opinions expressed by the justices were extensively footnoted and interpolated with references to former Court decisions, case law, historic documents, scholarly books and pithy quotes. It reads in places like a term paper prepared by fresh-faced law clerks—which in a sense it was.

By far the most long-winded opinion was written by Justice William Brennan, whose concurring arguments took up fully two thirds of the Court document. Brennan, among other things, reiterated—just in case the reader had somehow not gotten the point by then—

that religious exercises were unconstitutional because they did not serve a secular purpose. This dubious assertion was not only bad ideology, but also contradicted the opinion of Thomas Jefferson, to whom the justices frequently referred. Justice Arthur Goldberg's concurring opinion actually questioned the concept of secular neutrality but in the end he agreed with the majority decision.

The dissent of Justice Stewart is interesting in that it did not necessarily disagree with the majority decision. Stewart was concerned that the case had not been given a thorough enough hearing. His preference was to have additional debate. For Stewart the key issue was coercion, and he was not sure that the Baltimore school district had coerced me into acknowledging any kind of religious belief. If laws are responsive to the community, can be changed if parents complain, and if there are desirable options for dissenters, then, according to Stewart, the law is neither coercive nor unconstitutional. He thought the case turned on this point. If a state passed a law that was coercive with regard to religion, it was unconstitutional; if not, no harm was done. Stewart concluded that not enough evidence had been presented and no judgment was possible under those circumstances.

There are a few other key concepts in the decision. One is the relationship between the establishment and free exercise clauses of the First Amendment. "Congress shall make no law respecting the establishment of religion, or prohibiting the free exercise thereof;..." These clauses were intended by the framers to be in agreement, pointing toward one goal. As Goldberg wrote in his concurring opinion, "These two proscriptions are to be read together, and in light of a single end which they are designed to serve. The basic purpose of the religion clauses in the First Amendment is to promote and assure the fullest possible scope of religious liberty and tolerance for all, and to nurture the conditions which secure the best hope of attainment of that end."

For example, a law requiring the use of the Episcopal prayer book in all church services would be unconstitutional because it would constitute both an establishment of religion and a prohibition against the free exercise thereof by non-Episcopalians. But these two clauses have come into conflict in recent decades, and as Justice Stewart wrote in his dissent, "There are areas where a doctrinaire reading of the Establishment Clause leads to irreconcilable conflict with the Free Exercise Clause." For example, the employment by the government of chaplains in the U.S. armed services, strictly interpreted, would seem to constitute a violation of the establishment clause.

Brennan explains this issue in his concurring opinion. "It is argued that such provisions may be assumed to contravene the Establishment Clause, yet be sustained on constitutional grounds as necessary to secure to the members of the Armed Services ... those rights of worship guaranteed under the Free Exercise Clause. Since government has deprived such persons of the opportunity to practice their faith at places of their choice, the argument runs, government may, in order to avoid infringing the free exercise guarantees, provide substitutes where it requires such persons to be." The interpretation of the two religion clauses of the First Amendment is a delicate matter requiring sound judgment and an eye to the framers' intent, because a doctrinaire reading quickly leads to logical contradiction and legal paralysis.

The Court's interpretation of the rights guaranteed by these two clauses has given rise to useful, if not strictly constitutional, language. In deciding what laws are allowed and what laws are prohibited, the Court used the terms "neutrality" toward religion and the "separation" of church and state. These are often defined as the prohibition of government from giving aid to particular religions or religion in general, and the necessity for the state to avoid too much "involvement" or "entanglement." However, separation is a concept that should be used with care. "Separation of church and state" is a phrase borrowed from Thomas Jefferson. Nevertheless, its use here is not an appropriate one. In fact, Jefferson himself did *not* advocate separation of church and state as a hard and fast rule. The First Amendment was only intended to separate church and state in the most obvious and plain sense; it was not intended to be a comprehensive ban on all interaction between civic and spiritual life. In his dissent, Stewart noted—disapprovingly and with a hint of grumpiness— the Court's "ritualistic invocation of the nonconstitutional phrase 'separation of church and state.'" As he suggested, we should not confuse the phrase with the words of the First Amendment.

"Neutrality" toward religion, on the other hand, is probably the best one-word description of the intent of the First Amendment. It is a worthy goal for government and a sound interpretation of the two clauses, but the concept of neutrality is a slippery one. The Court thought that banning school prayer was tantamount to taking a neutral stance toward religion. I disagree. I think the Court privileged a secular value system and its stance was overwhelmingly hostile to religion. Let us look at one way in which the Court articulated its neutrality. The Court's decision claimed that government cannot "pass laws that aid one religion, aid all religions, or prefer one religion over another." Even if we affirm the Court's attitude, is it "aid" if the government does nothing more than allow children to pray? I think not. The idea of neutrality is difficult because it means different things to different people.

The concept of neutrality, as the Court defined it, is inadequate. Neutrality was equated with secularism. The Court explicitly advocated secularism as the preferred "neutral," value-free, "safe" approach to education. The decision said, "That is to say that to withstand the strictures of the Establishment Clause *there must be a secular legislative purpose* and a primary effect that neither advances nor inhibits religion." But we know that secularism is decidedly not value free; it is one system in competition with many. And so the Court's definition of neutrality falls apart at the center. It is undermined because it is neutral only from a particular, biased perspective.

So what are we to do in the face of several competing notions of neutrality? A universal concept is impossible. One person's neutrality is another's religion. When we try to define it closely, the concept always breaks down. Therefore, we must redefine neutrality and build in a certain degree of flexibility that allows for regional differences. We must ask the question "Whose neutrality?" The logical answer is more local control. School districts should be entitled to negotiate their own definition. This position is far more defensible and has its roots in the earliest conception of American democracy. Jefferson himself advocated locally organized public schools called wards or hundreds. Distributing power to the people, checked in broad terms by the courts, was Jefferson's original vision.

The distinction between "sectarian" and "religious" seems barely to have registered with the Court. The justices repeatedly criticized as unacceptable the *sectarian* nature of Bible reading but argued that because the exercises were *religious* they had to go. Throughout the decision these two terms are conflated. Goldberg and Justice John Harlan, for example, made a logical leap that the whole Court seemed to adopt. They wrote that the practices codified in the Baltimore law were unconstitutional because "they involve the state so significantly and directly in the realm of the sectarian as to give rise to those very divisive influences and inhibitions of freedom which both religion clauses of the First Amendment preclude. The state has ordained and utilized its facilities to engage in unmistakably religious exercises...." Notice that the justices substituted the word "religious" in the second sentence for the word "sectarian" in the first. I want to insist on the difference, but only to say that allowing religious exercises in general is different from endorsing a particular sectarian practice. Indeed, one is constitutional while the other is not.

Perhaps the most important issue is *coercion*. Coercing a student into engaging in a particular sectarian practice is clearly unconstitutional. But the general promotion of religion as an alternative to secularism is a different thing. The nature of coercion when applied to schools is a delicate issue because we are dealing with children and not adults. Stewart is the only justice who saw this issue clearly. Other justices mentioned it, but were so taken by the obvious establishment issue, they did not give it much attention.

Stewart wrote, "It is clear that the dangers of coercion involved in the holding of religious exercises in a schoolroom differ qualitatively from those presented by the use of similar exercises or affirmations in ceremonies attended by adults. Even with children, however, the duty of government in connection with religious exercises in the public schools, is that of refraining from so structuring the school environment as to put any kind of pressure on a child to participate in those exercises; it is not that of providing an atmosphere in which children are kept scrupulously insulated from any awareness that some of their fellows may want to open the school day with prayer, or of the fact that there exist in our pluralistic society differences of religious belief." I think Stewart got it right. He recognized the problem and acknowledged that children should not be isolated from the fact that they are different. However, the Court's idea of education did not affirm the founders' belief that children need to be taught citizenship in a context of religious values.

# A Little History

The Supreme Court's decision on school prayer was about history as well as law. Of course the justices went to considerable lengths to rehearse the relevant precedents and case law in their decision, but the bulk of the document was concerned with the people and events of our nation's past. Whenever matters of history are involved, additional criteria have to be taken into account. When lawyers engage in historical analysis they operate under rules shared by other disciplines. The justices performed a task similar to that of a theologian interpreting Scripture. The Constitution and the Bill of Rights were the texts entrusted to them. They were the priesthood of a "sacred" tradition. The documents to which they referred, and were expected to interpret, are enshrined like holy writ in the National Archives, as ancient texts of Scripture are in the Vatican

Library and the British Museum. Hearings were held in a templelike building. The justices wore vestments. And just as theologians are expected to engage in meticulous historical-critical analyses of the Bible, we expected the justices to use stringent standards when they interpreted the canons of American democracy. But did they?

Historians typically subject their documentary sources to a whole series of painstaking investigations. How well did the justices represent the intentions of the founders? This is a relevant question because the founders are invoked as proof of the need to ban prayer from public schools. Did the justices pay close attention to the narrative sources they quoted? Did they pick the most relevant documents or passages? Did they engage in good critical methods in an attempt to understand the meaning of the texts? Did they ascertain, as far as it was possible, the minds of the founders? Were they in sympathy with the motives of Jefferson, Madison, Williams, Locke and the other historical figures they cited? Did they discover the ideas behind the facts? These are questions that every American must ask. We cannot expect our justices to be masters of every discipline, experts at historiography, skilled social theorists, accomplished critical scholars. But we can expect them to represent fairly the intentions of the founding fathers. After all, these are not the works of obscure authors writing from antiquity on cuneiform tablets. The writings of the founders are available and accessible to everyone in America within range of a public library.

Let us take a look at that history for ourselves. In the decision, the justices said, "Nothing but the most telling of personal experiences in religious persecution suffered by our forebears … could have planted our belief in liberty of religious opinion any more deeply in our heritage." But who are our forebears in religious persecution? We learned in school that the Pilgrims landed at Plymouth Rock as religious refugees, but refugees from what?

The desire for tolerance and religious freedom in America has its roots in the experiences of religious dissidents in England. If we are to understand the meaning of the First Amendment, we must first look at the history of religious repression in that country.

The story really begins in the sixteenth century with the irascible king who wanted a divorce so badly he started his own church to get it: Henry VIII. The Protestant Reformation did not come to England as it had in Europe. There was no English equivalent to Martin Luther; no ninety-five theses were nailed to the doors of Westminster Abbey. In England, it was a victory of libido over Roman liturgy. Protestantism was embraced as a result of Henry's desire for an heir. Unable to secure the pope's blessing to divorce his wife, Henry broke with the Roman Church. And then, as we learned in high school, he beheaded a succession of brides. But, as most of us failed to learn, the nuptial bloodshed that characterized Henry's reign only foreshadowed the even bloodier history of religious persecution that followed. England had never been particularly tolerant under Roman Catholicism, but after the great schism between Canterbury and Rome, things got worse. Henry and his successors struggled violently over whether Catholicism or Anglicanism would rule the nation. The pendulum swung several times.

In the end, the Anglicans won, if only by virtue of the fact that Elizabeth I, an Anglican and one of Henry's successors, outlasted her rivals. But it was a costly victory. The circumstances were ghastly for the poor citizens of England, and the struggle for religious power was full of cruel ironies. In the battle for control, church and state each used the peculiar weapons at its disposal. The pope excommunicated the queen and absolved her subjects from allegiance. The queen decreed that loyalty to the pope was treason. The church-state calculus went something like this: Embrace the queen and rot in hell/embrace the pope and rot in jail. Is it any wonder that many of the queen's subjects, faced with this conundrum, chose an entirely different option? Henry VIII sowed the seeds of dissent and Elizabeth I watered them. The sixteenth and seventeenth centuries subsequently produced a never-ending stream of religious dissidents, among them the Puritans and the Separatists. Both wanted change, but of a different nature. The Puritans were reformers and the Separatists were revolutionaries. The Puritans thought the Church of England was too "popish" and wanted to "purify" it by simplifying the liturgy and making it more explicitly Bible centered. The Separatists wanted to be free of the Anglican Church altogether.

As dissent grew, Elizabeth responded to the "varieties, novelties, and diversities" that were disturbing the "ordered ceremonial" of the church by directing Archbishop Matthew Parker, in March of 1566, to issue "advertisements" prohibiting ministers from preaching without a license from an Anglican bishop. This drove dissenting pastors underground and helped create a system of small, secret churches called conventicles. These churches were hunted down by government agents and informers, and many of their members were jailed. Yet even those who were properly licensed came under state scrutiny. Licensed rural clergy, who gathered in market towns for Bible meetings, were surveilled. Their convocations, open to the public and a primary means of education for laypeople, were considered a threat. An opening prayer at such an event was considered an initiating gesture to an act of subversion. Consequently, the number of licensed preachers was arbitrarily reduced by order of the government to three or four per county. The meetings were effectively quashed.

The man responsible for the conditions that brought about the Pilgrims' flight to America was the infamous appointee of Elizabeth I, Archbishop John Whitgift. In the 1580s, Whitgift and his minions tirelessly pursued religious dissidents, among them the London Separatists led by John Greenwood and Henry Barrow. By March 1593, the Separatists filed a petition complaining that "threescore and twelve persons," men and women, young and old, lying in cold, hunger, dungeons, and irons [have been] "denied meat, fire and drink." Many had died "in the same noisome gaols...." The coffin of one who died in prison, Roger Rippon, was sent to the house of the judge who had sentenced him. An inscription on the lid read, "One of the last sixteen or seventeen which that great enemy of God, the Archbishop of Canterbury, with his high [state] commissioners, have murdered in Newgate [prison]...." In 1620, feeling the heat of persecution, the first Pilgrims left for the colonies. John Robinson's separatist church, the Leiden Congregation, sailed for Plymouth, Massachusetts. Many more were to follow. By 1640, the Massachusetts Bay Colony had a population of twenty thousand.

The political climate in England continued to be stormy throughout the seventeenth century, but the one constant was religious persecution. Through a long succession of power struggles and political adjustments, the dreary pageant of public floggings, hangings, imprisonment and torture continued. In spite of many differences, the crown and Parliament agreed on one principle: Religion was the legitimate subject of state control. As a result, a whole series of official acts defined and proscribed the limits of religious expression. The Corporation Act of 1661 restricted local political office to Anglicans in good standing. The Uniformity Act of 1662 required subscription by the clergy to the Anglican prayer book, the Thirty-nine Articles (a statement of doctrine), and the swearing of an oath to Anglican supremacy and the crown. This act resulted in the expulsion of nearly twenty thousand ministers, about 20 percent of all the clergy in England. The Conventicle Act of 1664, aimed at the Puritans, barred them from assembling in groups of more than five persons. The Five Mile Act of 1665 made it illegal for excluded clergy to come within five miles of their former places of worship. Finally, the Test Act of 1673 required every public officeholder to take Anglican communion and denounce the doctrine of transubstantiation. This excluded all Catholics and dissenters from civil or military office. England's Test Act was administered well into the eighteenth century and not officially repealed until the 1860s. The founding fathers found this act odious and Article VI of our Constitution was a direct response to it: "No religious Test shall ever be required as a Qualification to any Office or public Trust under the United States."

As in the past, people who wish to pray these days in public schools and institutions must sometimes resort to highly creative strategies. Although they may not know it, such tactics have a long tradition. English dissenters, in order to avoid arrest, employed a wide variety of devices and diversions. Presbyterians used to hold services under the ruse of a party or feast, and if discovered by the authorities, "would put up their Bibles" and turn their attention to "tobacco pipes, flagons of drink, cold meat, bread and cheese." Congregationalists would meet at "two or three o'clock in the morning" or in an attic above the meetinghouse. One dissident preacher held services on a rock in the middle of the Kingsbridge estuary at low tide. At another congregation, "several women big with child" obstructed the entrance, trusting that "male chivalry" would prevent authorities from removing them by force. In the countryside, Joseph Oddy preached in the woods at night, seated on horseback, poised for a quick escape. The minister of the Broadmore Baptists spoke from behind a curtain, preventing any informer who might slip into the congregation from recognizing him. John Flavell exploited the lack of cooperation between competing jurisdictions and preached at a point where three counties converged. When the constables from one jurisdiction approached, he would step into another county and avoid arrest.

Although these strategies were sometimes humorous, they had a serious purpose. Religious uniformity was enforced with malice and brutality. According to the Conventicle Act, the property of dissenters was subject to confiscation. Professional informers amassed large sums of money by turning people in. Meetings, if discovered, were broken up by soldiers "beating and kicking and hurling people on heaps and pushing them with the ends of their muskets." Even the smallest act could have expensive consequences. Edmund Tucker, a preacher who had been ejected from the clergy for nonconformance, was fined a substantial sum "for praying with three gentlewomen who came to visit his wife, and comfort her upon the death of her son...." No act was too small to merit the avarice of petty magistrates and bureaucrats. If one was unlucky enough to be sent to gaol, it was much worse. The prisons of the day were stinking holes. "The filthy, congested, foul-smelling,

Restoration gaols" were described as "unheated in winter and sweltering in summer, the breeding-ground of fever, plague and smallpox...." Yet people persisted in their prayers and religious meetings. By 1688, the situation was so bad that something had to be done. There were not enough jails and magistrates in England to keep the dissidents under control. William and Mary, the reigning monarchs, issued an edict granting limited freedoms to dissenters.

William and Mary's edict was followed promptly by the Toleration Act of 1689. It was a step in the right direction. The act still required oaths of allegiance and supremacy, but established a process by which dissenters could apply for a license to meet. Nonconforming ministers, if they agreed to certain state-defined religious principles, could be exempted from the Uniformity Act and the Five Mile Act. Baptists were excused from the legal obligation to engage in infant baptism and Quakers were allowed to make a "declaration" of allegiance instead of an "oath" (Quakers thought it "unscriptural" to take an oath). But the act required everyone to affirm the doctrine of the trinity and explicitly excluded Roman Catholics and Unitarians. Furthermore, dissenters were not granted civil equality and were barred from entering public service. Catholics were not officially emancipated until the Roman Catholic Emancipation Act of 1829. The state loosened its grip a little, but kept its hand firmly on the wheel.

The Toleration Act was a pragmatic response to acute political and social unrest. It was an incomplete solution full of loopholes. It was unclear, for example, whether it granted freedom of dissent to those who taught in religious schools and academies. School-masters could still be prosecuted in civil court for teaching without "an episcopal license," and in the early eighteenth century, controversies arose over this issue. In 1714, Parliament passed a bill to "prevent the growth of schism" by forbidding anyone who had attended a dissenting congregation from teaching in a recognized school or academy. The penalty for doing so was three months in prison. This was a measure aimed squarely at destroying the ability of dissenters to perpetuate themselves through an educated clergy. Three years earlier the Bill for Preventing Occasional Conformity had been passed. It intended to weed out those who were orthodox in their public life but who worshiped in dissenting churches privately. And so the English government continued to meddle in religious affairs well into the nineteenth century.

The Supreme Court said in its majority opinion, "It is true that [religious] liberty frequently was not realized by the colonists, but this is readily accountable by their close ties to the Mother Country." Most of America's early settlers were religious dissidents fleeing persecution in order to establish their own communities where they could worship without interference. With this in mind, it should not come as a complete surprise that Americans institutionalized religious freedoms in the Constitution. But religious liberty did not arrive in America on the decks of the *Mayflower*. And the religious attitudes of the colonists went far deeper than their "close ties" to England. The early colonists had no intention of establishing religious freedom and, in fact, established their own unique varieties of religious intolerance. The early colonists were not secular people. Their entire outlook on the world was religious. It was inconceivable to them that any form of government could be established on these shores in which religion did not play a role. The colonists were only interested in sectarian freedom—the right to pursue the religious polity of their own sect. Church and state were completely conflated in the thinking of the Pilgrims. The religious intolerance of the early colonists was not the result of a political or administrative link to England; it was a matter of worldview. The genius of the founding fathers was in their ability to break through this old paradigm.

> Let men of God in court and churches watch
> O'er such as do a toleration hatch.
> > —THOMAS DUDLEY, 1653
> > Governor of Massachusetts Bay Colony

Religious tolerance was not widely established in America for more than a century after the first Pilgrims arrived at Plymouth. The ditty, found in Governor Dudley's pocket at the time of his death, reflected the prevailing political wisdom. With one exception, all of the original colonies were intolerant of religious difference.

The original Pilgrims in Plymouth, and especially those who settled farther north in Salem, established communities that were as strict and intolerant as the England they had fled. The settlers who colonized the Massachusetts Bay Colony in Salem were notorious for their rigid and strictly enforced code of living. But however inconsistent their persecution may seem to us today, the first settlers were, in fact, quite consistent. They did not believe in tolerance. The majority of the first Pilgrims never questioned the union of church and state. Dewey Wallace, in his history of the Pilgrims wrote, "It is sometimes claimed that the Puritans were inconsistent in fleeing England because of religious persecution and then becoming persecutors themselves, but however deplorable to the modern mind their behavior may seem, it was not inconsistent: they had not even when persecuted in England maintained that the established church ought not to suppress heresy but only that it was mistaken in persecuting them since they were not in error."

In fact, the Puritans considered themselves the New England branch of the Anglican Church. They simply had a different, "correct," view of true religion: simple, austere, Scripture centered and less dependent on tradition. They did not consider their flight to America an act of separatism. They intended to be the Church of England on a foreign shore, the Church rightly reformed and conformed to the Word of God. In their opinion the Anglican Church was tainted by compromise and married to an old order that prevented the realization of a true "holy commonwealth." Colonization offered them the opportunity to shape a reformed church, without threat or interference from a hostile state and without being forced to embrace separatism. Consequently, both civil and religious matters were combined and codified into their charter:

### Charter of the Massachusetts Bay, March 4, 1629

CHARLES, BY THE GRACE OF GOD, Kinge of England, Scotland, Fraunce, and Ireland, Defendor of the Fayth, &c. TO ALL to whome theis Presents shall come Greeting...

...whereby our said People, Inhabitants there, may be soe religiously, peaceablie, and civilly governed, as their good Life and orderlie Conversacon, maie wynn and incite the Natives of Country, to the Knowledge and Obedience of the onlie true God and Sauior of Mankinde, and the Christian Fayth, which in our Royall Intencon, and the Adventurers free Profession, is the principall Ende of this Plantacion.

The right of the government to enforce matters of religion was written into the bylaws. The Pilgrims were explicit about the power of civil magistrates to enforce religious polity. The document lists some religious "crimes," along with their appropriate punishments.

### Massachusetts Body of Liberties, December 10, 1641

A Coppie of the Liberties of the Massachusetts Colonie in New England.

Civill Authoritie hath power and libertie to see the peace, ordinances and Rules of Christ observed in every church according to his word. [S]o it be done in a Civill and not in an Ecclesiastical way.

If any man after legall conviction shall have or worship any other god, but the lord god, he shall be put to death.

If any man or woeman be a witch (that is hath or consulteth with a familiar spirit,) They shall be put to death.

If any man shall Blaspheme the name of god, the

father, Sonne or Holie ghost, with direct, expresse, presumptuous or high handed blasphemie, or shall curse god in the like manner, he shall be put to death.

John Winthrop emigrated to the Massachusetts Bay Colony and became governor in 1629. He wrote a pamphlet in 1644 entitled *A Short Story of the Rise, reign, and ruin of the Antinomiams, Familists & Libertines, that infected the Churches of New England*. It recounts the trials in 1636 of several heretics—including that of the famous Anne Hutchinson—explaining their errors and chronicling the course of events. After many pages dedicated to refuting their arguments, he observed:

Although the Assembly of the Churches had confuted and condemned most of those new [religious] opinions which were sprung up amoungst us ... the leaders in those erroneous ways would not give in....
[I]t was conceived by the Magistrates, and others of the Country ... that the means which had been used [to suppress them] proving ineffectual, the case was now desperate.... [I]t was determined ... to suppress them by civil authority.

And they did; in the case of Anne Hutchinson, for example,

the Court saw now an inevitable necessity to rid her away, except wee would be guilty, not onely of our owne ruine, but also of the Gospel: so in the end the sentence of banishment was pronounced against her, and she was committed to the Marshall, till the Court should dispose of her.

Despite the fact that Massachusetts and other colonies were repressive theocracies, the issue of "liberty of conscience" was raised almost from the beginning in colonial America. The history of early New England written by Cotton Mather, *Magnalia Christi Americana,* first published in 1702, records that five years after Winthrop's pamphlet:

> ...a bill was preferred unto the general court ... for the calling of a synod, whereby, a platform of church discipline, according to the direction of our Lord Jesus Christ in his blessed word, might most advantageously be composed and published. The magistrates in the general court passed the bill, but the deputies had their little scruples how far the civil authority might interpose in matters of such religious and ecclesiastical cognizance; and whether scaffolds might not now be raised, by the means whereof the civil authority should pretend hereafter to impose an uniformity, in such instances which had better be left at liberty and variety. It was reply'd, that it belong'd unto magistrates by all rational ways to encourage truth and peace among their people; and that the council now called by the magistrates was to proceed but by way of council, with the best light which could be fetched from the word of God; but the court would be after all free, as they saw cause to approve or to reject what should be offered.

Mather, not exactly a civil libertarian, and the instigator of the infamous Salem witch trials, could hardly hide his own love of strict religious discipline. He certainly approved, in retrospect, the idea of a religious council to advise the courts concerning their decisions. As we shall see later, this is precisely the kind of arrangement that an Englishman, John Locke, was criticizing: "[I]t is worthy to be observed and lamented that the most violent of these defenders of the truth, the opposers of errors, the exclaimers against schism do hardly ever let loose this their zeal for God, with which they are so warmed and inflamed, unless where they have the civil magistrate on their side. But so soon as ever court favor has given them the better end of the staff, and they begin to feel themselves the stronger, then presently peace and charity are to be laid aside."

But Mather, aware of the nascent toleration movement, reflected on the history of the Massachusetts colony with a jaundiced eye: "But certain persons, come lately from England, so inflamed the zeal for 'liberty of conscience' among the people, that all this compliance of the authority could not remove the fear of some churches, lest some invasion of that liberty were threatened by a clause in the order of the court, which intimated 'that what should be presented by the synod, the court would give such allowance as would be meet unto it.'"

Indeed, some churches were worried about the abuse of power and feared the synod's advisory power would be so influential that it would be equal to the authority of the civil court. The church of Boston, where many of the "heretics" John Winthrop described came from, was particularly concerned. But their objections to the convening of a synod were not ultimately persuasive. Those who favored the separation of civil and religious authority were very much in the minority. The synod was convened and in its first act it passed this resolution:

### *A Proposition about the Magistrate's Power in Matters of Religion*

The civil magistrate in matters of religion, or of the first table, hath power civilly to command or forbid things respecting the outward man which are clearly commanded or forbidden in the word, and to inflict suitable punishments, according to the nature of the transgression against the same.

Cotton Mather's opinion of "liberty of conscience" was typical of many early American colonists. He did not like it. Mather believed in the old, time-tested assertion that liberty of conscience implied only the freedom to respond to the truth—and nothing more. As far as he was concerned, holding a "false" opinion was not freedom but "bondage to error." He knew that a person in error could not be forced to believe anything, but that did not remove the civil necessity to restrain that person from "blaspheming the truth" and leading others into error. Mather, of course, had the hubris to assume he knew the truth. And while he represented the prevailing opinion, it was not a completely universal one.

Not every colony was as strict as Massachusetts. Some showed genuine signs of toleration. Pennsylvania was settled by Quakers, a group that had been terribly persecuted. Pennsylvania extended religious liberty to all who would acknowledge God, although "only those professing Christ as the Savior of the world and promising allegiance to the king and proprietor" were allowed to take part in government. Maryland passed the first official act of religious toleration in 1649, the Maryland Toleration Act. It was an act of self-defense on the part of Catholic settlers, who were becoming outnumbered. But it ultimately failed when the Anglican Church gained power and deprived the Catholics of their political rights.

The justices invoked the name of a little-known and early advocate of religious freedom, Roger Williams. "[T]he views of Madison and Jefferson, preceded by Roger Williams, came to be incorporated not only in the Federal Constitution but likewise in those of most of our states." Although most of the colonies eventually acquiesced on the issue of religious tolerance, for the most part, they resisted it. Of all the colonies, Rhode Island was the most tolerant of religious difference. It was established by an extreme Puritan, Roger Williams.

Williams was a clergyman and religious zealot. Because of his unorthodox opinions, he was driven from England in 1630 and settled in Boston. Williams had a talent for irritating church authorities. In Boston he refused to join the church because it would not make "public repentance" for having been in communion with the Church of England. He left Boston and went to Salem. There he got into trouble for denying the right of civil magistrates to punish sabbath breaking. He then left Salem and took refuge in Plymouth. Equally unpopular in Plymouth, he returned to Salem a second time—where he was banished. Governor Winthrop recorded the event: "Mr. Hooker was chosen to dispute with [Williams], but could not reduce him from any of his errors. So, the next morning the Court sentenced him to depart out of our jurisdiction within six weeks…"

As a last resort, Williams made his way to the shores of Narragansett Bay in Rhode Island, purchased land from the Indians and founded the settlement of Providence. There he started a colony that was, from the beginning, based on freedom of conscience. In 1638, when the settlement had grown large enough to require some form of government, they drew up a compact. It was signed by thirteen persons.

> We whose names are hereunder-written, being desirous to inhabit the town of Providence, do promise to submit ourselves, in active or passive obedience, to all such orders or agreements as shall be made for public good of the body, in an orderly way, by the major consent of the present inhabitants, masters of families incorporated together into a township, and such others whom they shall admit unto the same, only in civil things.

Succinct and to the point, this agreement was expanded and clarified in subsequent versions as the settlement grew. In 1641, in response to the steady immigration of "Newcomers," they drew up a document consisting of twelve articles. It included this phrase: "We agree, as formerly hath been the liberties of the town, so still, to hold forth liberty of conscience." A general court that convened in the same year passed a bill affirming that "it is ordered that the law of the last Court made concerning liberty of conscience in point of doctrine be perpetuated." Rhode Island soon grew large enough that its unusual liberties were threatened unless it became an official English colony. In 1643 and 1644, Williams traveled to England to seek a royal charter for the colony. In spite of the fact that England was at war, or perhaps because of it, he was successful. He was given a charter that granted the people of Rhode Island the freedom to organize a civil government as they saw fit. In 1647, an elected assembly met for the first time, agreed upon a form of government and drew up a code of law. The concluding words of the code contained this provision:

> These are the laws that concern all men, and these are the penalties for the transgressions thereof, which, by common consent, are ratified and established throughout the whole colony. And otherwise than thus, what is herein forbidden, all men may walk as their conscience persuade them, every one in the name of his God.

In other respects the charter was typical, but these words made it a milepost in Anglo-American history. That such radical freedom was achieved in 1647 is all the more to be admired because Williams was arguably a religious fanatic. He believed deeply in "one true religion," but he steadfastly refused to impose his will on others. He and his followers were amazingly progressive. Williams believed passionately in his own version of theological orthodoxy. He particularly disliked Quaker beliefs, and often disputed with them. In his book *George Fox Digged Out of His Burrowes*, Williams criticized them in bitter, sarcastic words he himself described as "sharp scripture language." Yet, despite his opinion, he defended them. While most of the colonies colluded in their persecution of the Quakers, bringing tremendous political pressure to bear, Rhode Island refused to do likewise. Meanwhile Massachusetts, with characteristic zeal, enacted capital laws against Quakers, hanging three men and one woman while mutilating and torturing others. Rhode Island, facing the threat of trade sanctions and the intervention of English authorities, responded with a letter:

> ...we may not be compelled to exercise any civil power over men's consciences, so long as human orders in point of civility are not corrupted and violated, which our neighbors about us do frequently practice, whereof many of us have large experience, and judge it to be no less than a point of Absolute Cruelty.

Williams wrote a significant body of work during his lifetime, and much of it advocated liberty of conscience. His most comprehensive and pointed work was *Confirmation of the Bloody Doctrine of Persecution for Cause of Conscience.* He wrote it while in England to seek the Rhode Island charter. In it he said, "[There is] a two-fold state, a civil state and spiritual state ... and being of different natures and considerations, as far differing as spirit from flesh, I first observe, that civil weapons are most improper and unfitting in matters of the spiritual state." But the most eloquent summary of his position was directed to Providence during its first expansion, before Rhode Island became a colony. The justices made reference to it in their decision. It was written in response to the claim that liberty of conscience would disrupt the civil peace. It is a classic statement of American tolerance:

> That ever I should write a tittle, that tends to such an

infinite liberty of conscience, is a mistake, and which I have ever disclaimed and abhorred. To prevent such mistakes, I shall at present only propose this case: There goes many a ship to sea with many hundred souls in one ship, whose weal and woe is common, and is a true picture of a commonwealth, or a human combination or society. It hath fallen out some times, that both papists and protestants, Jews and Turks, may be embarked in one ship; upon which supposal I affirm, that all the liberty of conscience, that I ever pleaded for, turns upon these two hinges—that none of the papists, protestants, Jews or Turks, be forced to come to ship's prayers or worship, nor compelled from their own particular prayers or worship, if they practice any. I further add that I never denied, that notwithstanding this liberty, the commander of this ship ought to command the ship's course, yea, and also command that justice, peace and sobriety, be kept and practiced both among seamen and all the passengers...

Justice Brennan, in the Court's position, made reference to one of the most influential forces in the American advance toward religious liberty, the writings of the English philosopher John Locke. "When John Locke ventured in 1689, 'I esteem it above all things to distinguish exactly the business of civil government from that of religion and to settle the just bounds that lie between the one and the other,' he anticipated the necessity which would be thought by the Framers to require adoption of a First Amendment, but not the difficulty that would be experienced in defining those 'just bounds.'" Justice Brennan was astute enough to recognize the importance of Locke, but his remark raises the question of how much he knew of Locke's educational philosophy.

Thomas Jefferson considered Locke one of the three greatest thinkers of all time. His writings deeply influenced our nation's early leaders, particularly the authors of the Constitution. Unknown to everyday Americans, Locke's ideas are essential to an understanding of the place of religion in government and education as it came to be conceived by the founders. Locke was raised in a strict Puritan household with strong Parliamentarian (as opposed to Royalist) leanings. Religious dissent and progressive politics marked his formative years. Locke was enormously gifted, wrote extensively and is usually credited with opening the period of intellectual renewal in England known as the Enlightenment. His main work of philosophy was *Essay Concerning Human Understanding.* It is almost impossible to underestimate the impact of Locke and Enlightenment thinking on the architects of the new American democracy.

Locke was famous among the founding fathers for his political writings. He and his fellow Enlightenment thinkers ushered in a new era of progressive thought and subjected the whole variety of human endeavor and institutions to a new "light of reason." The intellectual movement he started played a vital role in the new and developing doctrine of church-state separation in America. Locke's ideas, so natural sounding to us, were radical in his day. In his book *Concerning Civil Government,* he proposed the idea that the state's only reason for existence was to protect "life, liberty, health and indolency of body" (words echoed in the Declaration of Independence) and its only sovereignty was that derived from those governed. He argued that kings did not rule by divine right or by virtue of their royal birth; they ruled by the consent of the governed. These ideas did not make him popular with the monarchy in England, but his theories were deeply admired by Thomas Jefferson and many others in America. When it came time to write the Declaration of Independence, Jefferson borrowed many ideas and words from Locke: "We hold these Truths to be self-evident, that all Men are created equal, that they are endowed by their Creator with certain unalienable Rights, that among these are Life, Liberty, and the Pursuit of Happiness." Apparently Jefferson, like most Americans, did not know what "indolency of body" meant either.

Just as Locke's ideas about the locus of authority and the limits of power came to be admired by Americans, so would his opinions about the proper relationship of church and state. Locke was among the first in England to argue for religious toleration, but not the very first. That honor may go to John Smyth. Smyth was a Separatist who in his early years had no objection to the idea of state-enforced religion. He was a priest in the Church of England until 1606 but became the founder of organized Baptist churches in England. After years of severe persecution he came to believe that government had no right to interfere in matters of religion. This was a radical belief in his day and opinions like his were extremely rare. He wrote in

1612: "The magistrate is not by virtue of his office to meddle with religion, or matters of conscience, to force and compel men to this or that form of religion or doctrine: but to leave Christian religion free, to every man's conscience, and to handle only civil transgressions, injuries, and wrongs of men against men." Smyth's concept of tolerance, however, was limited to Christians.

Another lonely voice for tolerance was that of Leonard Busher, a member of a Baptist congregation, who published a tract in 1614. The tolerance he advocated was considerably more wide ranging than Smyth's.

> As kings and bishops cannot command the wind, so they cannot command faith, and as the wind bloweth where it listeth, so is every man that is born of the Spirit. You may force men to church against their consciences, but they will believe as they did before, when they come there.... I read that Jews, Christians and Turks are tolerated in Constantinople, and yet are peaceable, though so contrary the one to the other. If this be so how much more ought Christians not to force one another to religion! And how much more ought Christians to tolerate Christians, when as the Turks do tolerate them! Shall we [be] less merciful than the Turks?...

In spite of the homespun earnestness of pleas like Busher's, it took a man of Locke's insight to extend the concept of toleration and provide the intellectual muscle and empiricist methodology. Like Smyth and Busher, Locke was a dedicated Christian and had even written an "apology" entitled *The Reasonableness of*

*Christianity.* But he had a broader vision of toleration. His essay *A Letter Concerning Toleration* articulated his views and became one of the most famous essays ever written. Locke believed that the government, whose instrument he called the "magistrate," should refrain from any attempt to control matters of religion.

> The commonwealth seems to me to be a society of men constituted only for procuring, preserving, and advancing their own civil interests. Civil interests I call life, liberty, health, and indolency of body; and the possession of outward things, such as money, land, houses, furniture, and the like. It is the duty of the civil magistrate, by the impartial execution of equal laws, to secure unto all the people in general and to every one of his subjects in particular the just possession of these things belonging to his life.... Now that the whole jurisdiction of the magistrate reaches only to these civil concernments, and that all civil power, right and dominion, is bounded and confined to the only care of promoting these things; and it neither can nor ought in any manner to be extended to the salvation of souls, these following considerations seem unto me abundantly to demonstrate.

Locke argued that the state's primary tool is force, and because force can only compel public conformity, it can never coerce people into actually changing their minds. "The care of souls cannot belong to the civil magistrate, because his power consists only in outward force; but true and saving religion consists in the inward persuasion of the mind, without which nothing can be acceptable to God. And such is the nature of the understanding, that it cannot be compelled by outward force." Locke's essay was remarkable. It called on magistrates and ordinary citizens, of whatever religious faith, to exercise tolerance. He extended this civic right even to those who were not Christians—a magnanimous gesture for the time. "No private person has any right in any manner to prejudice another person in his civil enjoyments because he is of another church or religion. All the rights and franchises that belong to him as a man, or as a denizen, are inviolably to be preserved to him. These are not the business of religion. No violence nor injury is to be offered him, whether he be Christian or Pagan."

Locke's views were not popular in government circles. He and his friends, in particular the earl of Shaftsbury, were considered seditious by the state. The *Letter Concerning Toleration* was written in exile as Locke had fled to Holland in 1683 and published it there in Latin. It was not widely circulated, however, until the English version was issued when he returned home. The issue of religious freedom held great importance for him all his life but it also embroiled him in endless controversy. The letter had many detractors who argued along with the government that only those who embraced "true religion" should be respected. His response was characteristically straightforward: "It will be answered, undoubtedly, that it is the orthodox church which has the right of authority over the erroneous or heretical. This is, in great and specious words, to say just nothing at all. For every church is orthodox to itself; to others, erroneous or heretical." Were there any limits to Locke's tolerance? Yes. He made an exception for atheists. "[Atheists] are not at all to be tolerated [because they] deny the being of God. Promises, covenants, and oaths, which are the bounds of human society, can have no hold upon an atheist." There are many strange ironies in the school prayer issue, but none more than this. As we have seen, the leading atheist in America was responsible for ushering in a new age of intolerance for religion.

# *Religion and Education*

[We believe] that the religion, or the duty which we owe to our Creator, and the manner of discharging it, can be directed only by reason and conviction, not by force or violence; and therefore all men are equally entitled to the free exercise of religion, according to the dictates of conscience.

> —THOMAS JEFFERSON
> Virginia Declaration of Rights
> June 12, 1776

The Supreme Court said in its decision, "Religious freedom was first in the forefathers' minds; it was set forth in absolute terms, and its strength is its rigidity." Yet we know that religious liberty was neither embraced by many early colonists nor by a few of Jefferson's contemporaries. Nevertheless, by the latter part of the eighteenth century, much had changed in America. As we have seen, Roger Williams and the Rhode Island colony were early leaders in the fight for religious tolerance. But the "otherwise-minded" colony never exerted much political clout and had little influence on the other colonies. Another commonwealth, one of the most influential, would lead the way in preparing for the new religious freedoms enshrined in the Constitution and Bill of Rights. That state was Virginia, and its two most famous residents were James Madison and Thomas Jefferson.

In the 1760s and early 1770s, the relationship between the American colonies and England, always strained, began to come apart. Draconian restrictions on American trade known as the Intolerable Acts had been passed by Parliament and led to the famous Boston Tea Party, the revolutionary slogan "No taxation without representation" and eventually the first Continental Congress. By 1775, the conflict had escalated to armed clashes with British troops in Lexington and Concord. By 1776, the colonies were at war and on July Fourth, Jefferson's Declaration of Independence was published by the Second Continental Congress. The next five years were occupied by the war, and the Constitution was not approved until 1787. The Bill of Rights was ratified in 1791. The first sentence of the first of ten amendments in the Bill of Rights addressed the issue of religious freedom.

Virginia, under the leadership of Madison and Jefferson, led the way in the fight for religious freedom.

The Virginia Declaration of Rights, passed just days before the Declaration of Independence, was largely their work. Both men were Enlightenment thinkers and intellectual heirs of John Locke. The Episcopal Church (the Anglican Church in America) was the official church of Virginia and prior to the passage of the declaration, other churches were not granted official permission to hold services. In Virginia, the Episcopal Church was the state church and tax money supported the clergy. This marriage of church and state was firmly opposed by a long list of dissenters, including Baptists, Quakers and Presbyterians. In one of their petitions, called a memorial, the dissenters made this argument:

> Therefore we ask no ecclesiastical establishment for ourselves, neither can we approve of them and grant it to others; this, indeed, would be giving exclusive or separate emoluments or privileges to one set (or sect) of men, without any special public services, to the common reproach or injury of every other denomination. And, for the reasons recited, we are induced earnestly to entreat that all laws now in force in this commonwealth which countenance religious domination may be speedily repealed...

The various churches pushed the issue for several years until late 1784, when things came to a head. In that year legislation was introduced to the state assembly entitled A Bill Establishing a Provision for Teachers of the Christian Religion. The bill permitted a person to pay a tithe (an official tax) to any denomination—not just the Episcopal Church—or to a school. The bill was championed by Patrick Henry. It looked like progress, and in a sense it was, but Madison and Jefferson opposed it, fear-ing it did not go far enough and might impede the passage of a more wide-ranging bill. They objected, arguing that it privileged Christianity over other religions—a very radical idea. Madison managed to get a vote on the bill postponed and wrote his famous argument, A Memorial and Remonstrance Against Religious Assessments. Madison reasoned that any religious tax was "a dangerous abuse of power." He argued:

> [I]t is proper to take alarm at the first experiment on our liberties. We hold this prudent jealousy to be the first duty of Citizens, and one of the noblest characteristics of the late Revolution. The free men of America did not wait till usurped power had strengthened itself by exercise, and entangled the question in precedents. They saw all the consequences in the principle, and they avoided the consequences by denying the principle. We revere this lesson too much soon to forget it. *Who does not see that the same authority which can establish Christianity, in exclusion of all other Religions, may establish with the same ease any particular sect of Christians, in exclusion of all other Sects* [emphasis added]?

Madison's efforts were successful and the bill failed to pass. In its place Jefferson drafted A Bill for Establishing Religious Freedom, which granted complete religious freedom to every citizen of Virginia—Christians, Jews and pagans—and established the precedent that allowed for the repeal or "disestablishment" of the Episcopal Church soon thereafter. Jefferson, the consummate Enlightenment scholar, penned an eloquent tribute to religious liberty:

> ...Almighty God hath created the mind free, and

manifested his supreme will that free it shall remain by making it altogether insusceptible of restraint.

...the impious presumption of legislators and rulers, civil as well as ecclesiastical, who, being themselves but fallible and uninspired men, have assumed dominion over the faith of others, setting up their own opinions and modes of thinking as the only true and infallible...

...our civil rights have no dependence on our religious opinions, any more than our opinions in physics or geometry.

We the General Assembly of Virginia do enact that no man shall be compelled to frequent or support any religious worship, place, or ministry whatsoever, nor shall be enforced, restrained, molested, or burthened in his body or goods, nor shall otherwise suffer, on account of his religious opinions or belief; but that all men shall be free to profess, and by argument maintain, their opinions in matters of religion, and that the same shall in no wise diminish, enlarge, or affect their civil capacities.

The sentiment Jefferson expressed here was to be expressed again five years later in the Bill of Rights.

This chapter began with a quote from the Virginia Declaration of Rights. As originally drafted by George Mason it read, "All men should enjoy the fullest toleration in the exercise of religion." Madison successfully proposed an alternative, which read, "All men are equally entitled to the free exercise of religion." The distinction between these two phrases was an extremely important one to both Jefferson and Madison, and in this respect they advanced the cause of religious liberty beyond their forebears, including John Locke. By the time Madison wrote those words, his views about the nature of religious freedom had matured to the point where he thought toleration was an "invidious concept" because it implied that the state had the right to persecute religious nonconformists but chose not to. The founders wanted to advance beyond the concept of religious toleration to embrace the idea that everyone is granted an inviolable religious freedom. It is this idea of religious freedom the founders wrote into the Constitution.

Thomas Jefferson was in Paris campaigning by correspondence for a Bill of Rights when the Constitution was being written. He wrote to a friend, "I will now add what I do not like [about the Constitution]. First the omission of a bill of rights providing clearly, and without the aid of sophisms, for freedom of religion...." Jefferson lobbied so heavily by mail that he is credited with delaying ratification in several states. Madison attended the constitutional convention and at first opposed the idea on pragmatic grounds. He wanted to establish federal power as quickly as possible in the uncertain climate left after the Continental Congress but he later joined Jefferson in supporting the Bill of Rights. There were many suggestions for inclusion in it. New Hampshire, Virginia and New York adopted the Constitution but hoped that a declaration of religious freedom would be added. North Carolina and Rhode Island refused to accept the Constitution until they were reassured that a religious freedom amendment would be added later. At the first session of Congress, twelve amendments were approved, of which ten were ultimately ratified. Madison, the representative from Virginia, led the way. In the end, his propositions formed the basis for nearly all the approved amendments. It was Madison who worded the two religion clauses of the First Amendment:

> Congress shall make no law respecting an establishment of religion, or prohibiting the free exercise thereof; or abridging the freedom of speech, or of the press; or the right of the people peaceably to assemble, and to petition the Government for a redress of grievances.

These words have had a profound impact on religious life in this country and are the basis of the Supreme Court's decision on school prayer. Did the founders intend to apply the First Amendment to public education? We can begin to address that question by looking at the writings of John Locke. He was highly influential in Jefferson's thinking and among the first to argue for the separation of church and state. Did he advocate the removal of religion from civic life? Definitely not; neither did he think that prayer or religious studies were inappropriate in schools. In fact, he thought just the opposite. His intolerance of atheists, to which I have referred, was based on the belief that religious conviction of whatever kind was essential to a person's moral character, and moral character was essential to government.

Locke expressed his views on education and religion in several documents, among them an essay entitled *Of Study*. Written in 1677, it was printed and circulated fifty years later in Lord Peter King's *The Life of John Locke with Extracts from his Correspondence, Journals, and Common-Place Books.* Well known to Jefferson and others, these collected works revealed Locke's educational philosophy. In *Of Study,* he wrote: "Heaven being our great business and interest, the knowledge which may direct us thither is certainly so too; so that this is without peradventure the study which ought to take up the first and chiefest place in our thoughts." According to Locke, the most important task of education was religious instruction.

Shortly after Locke returned from exile in Holland, he received a letter from a friend, the Lady Mordaunt, asking for advice concerning the education of her oldest son. Locke wrote a thoughtful letter in return:

> With the reading of history I think the study of morality should be joined. I mean not the ethics of the Schools fitted to dispute, but ... [Cicero] ... and Aristotle, and above all the New Testament [which] teaches wherein a man may learn how to live...

Locke believed, as did all Enlightenment thinkers, in the importance of moral instruction for children. In another of his writings, *Some Thoughts Concerning Education,* he advocated teaching young children how to pray in school. In the essay Locke stated his educational philosophy unambiguously:

> Having laid the foundations of virtue in a true notion of God, such as the creed wisely teaches, as far as his age is capable, [teach] him to pray... ; [and] the next thing to be taken care of, is to keep him exactly to speaking the truth, and by all the ways imaginable inclining him to be good-natured.

Locke believed that parents and educators had the responsibility to teach children a concept of God as "the source of all good things to those that love and obey Him." For Locke, a person's conduct—both public and private—only became moral when it was based on the "laws of God." So while he wrote passionately in favor of the separation of church and state—and the toleration of all religions—he nevertheless strongly advocated religious training in the schools. Locke saw no inherent conflict of interest between church-state separation and education.

What about Thomas Jefferson? Did he intend the First Amendment to exclude religion from public education? No. There is nothing in any of Jefferson's writings to suggest this. In fact, Jefferson was not dogmatic about the separation of church and state. Remember, the phrase "separation of church and state" does not appear in the First Amendment—or anywhere else in the Constitution! It is true that the phrase "a wall of separation between church and State" comes from Jefferson, but it must be read in context. When taken out of context and represented as the sum total of Jefferson's thoughts about government and religion—as the Court has done time and again—we do a disservice to history. Jefferson wrote the phrase in question as president, in a letter to the Danbury Baptist Association, on January 1, 1802. He was responding to their request that he declare a day of fasting and thanksgiving. The paragraph containing the phrase reads:

> Believing with you that religion is a matter which lies solely between man and his God, that he owes

account to none other for his faith or worship, that the legislative powers of government reach actions only, and not opinions, I contemplate with sovereign reverence that act of the whole American People which declared that their legislature should "make no law respecting the establishment of religion, or prohibiting the free exercise thereof," *thus building a wall of separation between church and State* [emphasis added]. Adhering to this expression of the supreme will of the nation on behalf of the rights of conscience, I shall see with sincere satisfaction the progress of those sentiments which tend to restore to man all his natural rights, convinced he has no natural right in opposition to his social duties.

There are important things to note here. First, Jefferson was making a political decision, not a judgment on what was constitutional. If he was, he was an extremely inconsistent man because he contradicted himself on a number of occasions. Second, Jefferson knew very well that there were firm limits on the nature of his "wall of separation." He explicitly applied it to the legislature, which at the time meant *Congress only* and which certainly did not include public schools.

The main reason that limiting our study of Jefferson to this one document can lead to serious misinterpretation is that Jefferson was very flexible in his approach to religious liberty. It was *religious liberty* that he was committed to, not separation. He was willing to change his mind about the specific application of the First Amendment to suit a particular problem so long as it supported the ideal of religious freedom. In Jefferson's time, those needing protection were primarily

Christians outside state-sanctioned denominations and a few "pagans" and Jews. Today, those needing protection are Christians who want basic free-exercise rights to pray in school. Jefferson would not tolerate any hint of coercion, but school prayer is not inherently coercive.

Justice Brennan, in a footnote to his opinion, mentioned the work of Robert M. Healey, a Jefferson scholar. Healey published a book in 1962 entitled *Jefferson on Religion in Public Education,* which is an edited version of his doctoral dissertation at Yale. The footnote appears in this portion of Brennan's text: "But an awareness of history and an appreciation of the aims of the Founding Fathers do not always resolve concrete problems. The specific question before us has, for example, aroused vigorous dispute whether the architects of the First Amendment—James Madison and Thomas Jefferson particularly—understood the prohibition against any 'law respecting an establishment of religion' to reach devotional exercises in the public schools. It may be that [they] would have held such exercises to be permissible—although even in Jefferson's case serious doubt is suggested by his admonition against 'putting the Bible and Testament into the hands of the children at an age when their judgments are not sufficiently matured for religious inquiries' ... I doubt that their view ... would supply a dispositive answer to the question...." The contents of Healey's book, however, fail to establish much of a controversy. Jefferson's writings speak for themselves. In my opinion, Jefferson's thoughts are enormously useful in arriving at

a "dispositive answer." And the quote Brennan refers to
is out of context and hardly representative of his thinking. After going to some considerable trouble to but-
tress the majority opinion with historical references,
however, Brennan dismissed the entire corpus of
Jefferson's thoughts on education with a wave of the
hand.

Healey, in his exhaustive examination of Jefferson's
ideas on education, did not find any inherent conflict of
interest, and I am indebted to him for the following
observations. Jefferson knew that the limits of church-
state separation are variable and context specific.
Church members are never simply Christians but also
members of society. As such, they are entitled to all the
rights enjoyed by their fellow citizens without respect to
religious affiliation. If a particular religious organization
is removed from a position of direct government influence, free expression is promoted. But if members of
that same organization are prohibited from influencing
government in ways open to all other citizens, their
freedom is proscribed. Americans have tended to
believe that the opposite of religious persecution is
strict separation of church and state.

For Jefferson, constitutional limits were not absolutes
but means to an end—a government in which the will of
every citizen mattered. The doctrine of church-state
separation was intended to accomplish an end greater
than itself. Jefferson's chief interest was in establishing
religious freedom. He approached this ideal pragmati-
cally. He adapted the particular implementation of the
doctrine to a particular situation. He did not attempt to

define separation and then apply it politically. Rather, he tried to invent the best possible device to ensure freedom for whatever circumstances he encountered. If he felt a particular group was limiting freedom of opinion, he found it prudent to restrict members of such groups from public authority. When they ceased to exert undue power, he felt that they should be allowed to regain the exercise of their "natural" rights. The principle of separation could be relaxed where freedom of religious opinion did not threaten to disempower others. The doctrine was to be applied when it served to promote religious freedom and not otherwise, because the principle of church-state separation was no guarantee of religious freedom; too rigid an application of the principle can become religious persecution. It is important, therefore, to remember that Jefferson, who first used the words "wall of separation between church and State," also said, "I have sworn upon the altar of God, eternal hostility against every tyranny over the mind of man."

Jefferson knew that the church, even when separated from state powers, could ally with other forces, such as public opinion, to oppress. There was also the possibility that church-state separation might be used to persecute those who have religious beliefs by those who claim to have none. Jefferson recognized the government's responsibility to protect religious freedom of worship.

In fact, he wrote the Bill for Punishing Disturbers of Religious Worship and Sabbath Breakers and the Bill for Establishing Religious Freedom. These bills were intended to guarantee that worship services would not be subject to interference from public officials or private citizens. In other words, the government could not molest citizens in the peaceful expression of their religious beliefs or permit others to do so. Similar laws today have been criticized as violations of the principle of separation but this is not true. Jefferson's aim was not separation of church and state but the fullest possible freedom of belief and opinion.

First Amendment protections were important, but not foolproof. Like every other device Jefferson developed in his attempts to safeguard free government and individual liberty, it had to be applied intelligently by those it was designed to protect. It could only be effective for a citizenry who had tasted freedom and maintained it through vigilant supervision of state officials. Jefferson knew that Americans had loved freedom, and he had faith they would never willingly return to despotism. He also knew, however, that eternal vigilance could never be left to chance. Citizens had to be trained in the art of self-government. They had to learn how to discern the signs of the times and to act together in intelligent response to social needs. And for this problem there was only one solution—a system of public schools designed to develop in each person his or her fullest intellectual powers.

Jefferson was among the strongest and earliest advocates of universal public education. Like Locke before him, he was an educational theorist. He wrote letters of advice to many young men and women, and to their parents, about what they should read, in what order and where they should go to school. Jefferson thought that the most valuable part of education was the learning of morals. In his letters he repeatedly emphasized three important values to be achieved through education: morality, health and knowledge. He placed high importance on the "cultivation of virtue," the strengthening of the "moral sense" and the teaching of correct moral choices. He said in a letter to Peter Carr in 1785, "The defect of these virtues can never be made up by all the other acquirements of body and mind. Make these then, your first object. Give up money, give up fame, give up science, give up the earth itself and all it contains, rather than do an immoral act." To Jefferson the importance of religion in public education was the same as in private education: "to make men moral." Jefferson's educational philosophy was rooted in the ideal of a moral, healthy, capable person, independent and cooperative, whose worth was measured by industry and practical resourcefulness.

Jefferson believed that the goals of education were furthered by the teaching of "true religion" and inhibited by the teaching of dogmas or "religio-metaphysical abstractions." "True religion," for Jefferson, looked like this: "Eliminated from the field of public education would be exactly the doctrines which no one could agree [on] anyway." He said, "The said teacher shall, in all things relating to the education and government of their pupils, be under the direction and control of the Visitors; but no religious reading, instruction, or exercise, shall be prescribed or practiced inconsistent with the tenets of any religious sect or denomination."

Jefferson did not support the teaching of any particular denomination's dogma in public schools. This did not, however, mean the elimination of all religion in schools. For Jefferson, the elimination of "inconsistent tenets" or the dogma of a particular sect did not mean that religion was to be outlawed in public education any more than the prevention of state meddling in religious institutions meant that government was to be without religion. The purpose of the First Amendment was to guarantee and encourage religious freedom. This meant that those areas of religious belief that all sects agreed on were to be included within the framework of public education.

Jefferson thought, as have educators for millennia, that the primary aim of education was to produce a moral individual. All of Jefferson's proposals for religious instruction in public education were intended to attain this goal: the development of a moral citizen who would produce a moral society. And for Jefferson, morality was not fundamentally separable from religion. That is the key point. Jefferson wrote to John Adams in 1817 that religion "is more than an inner conviction of the existence of the Creator; true religion is morality ... the moral precepts, innate in man, and made part of his physical constitution, as necessary for his social being ... the sublime doctrines of philanthropism and deism taught us by Jesus of Nazareth, in which we all agree, constitute one religion." Given the inseparability of religion and morality, and given that education is about morality, it would be foolish and even dangerous to remove religion from schools.

Jefferson built room for disagreement into his vision of education in public schools. He was an advocate of community control and decision making. As long as no one's rights were violated, he thought the democratic process should flourish on every level. Jefferson believed that the American experiment in representative democracy made two conditions absolutely necessary: *local control* whenever possible and *public education to empower all citizens.* Jefferson campaigned to have school districts divided into "hundreds," or "wards," the ultimate units of a genuine democracy, and to institute a system of public education. He said, "I consider the continuance of republican government as absolutely hanging on these two hooks."

Reflecting on Jefferson's thoughts about education, Robert Healey made several observations:

1. *Our democratic form of government should be preserved and education is indispensable to that end.* Jefferson believed democracy to be a moral enterprise and the responsibility of schools was to educate moral citizens. The enemy of freedom is ignorance. The tendency of government is to encroach constantly on the rights of the people.

2. *Democracy should be rigid in principle but flexible in the implementation of those principles.* The doctrinaire application of the First Amendment to school prayer is a distortion of Jefferson's intent. He would have constructed the best compromise for any given situation. The school prayer decision was very uncompromising.

3. *A moral education is essential to the preservation of a democracy.* For Jefferson, the purpose of education was ineradicably moral. Healey says, "If we prove to our own satisfaction that science, technology, or a particular academic pursuit is neutral, amoral, divorced from the problem of choice, we have only ignored the fact that scientists, technologists, and students are men and can never be amoral."

4. *People are frightened by the passion of religious differences and have consequently pushed all religion out of public schools.* In schools where no compromise between contending groups has been possible, all vestiges of religion have been eliminated. This illusion of unity only hides intolerance.

5. *One goal of democracy is the recognition, solution and tolerance of controversy; public education should prepare citizens for this reality.* Healey says, "A community which refuses to admit the existence of conflict of opinion within its borders is a fool's paradise ... the role of religion in public education is to be determined by the need to make public education as effective a tool as possible in continuing and fostering the functioning of democracy and development of a free society ... to eliminate from public education the consideration of religion because it is controversial is to make that education defective as a training ground for democratic citizens."

Jefferson's ideas about religion and education are clear. What about other Americans? What did they think about the role of religion in the nation? In education?

Fortunately, we have a good account of American public opinion from an outside observer, Alexis de Tocqueville. Tocqueville, born in 1805, was a French historian who visited the United States with his friend Henri Beaumont in 1831, ostensibly to investigate the U.S. prison system. What he did, however, was publish a penetrating political study of the United States entitled *Democracy in America.* Tocqueville's visit coincided with the change of generations as the last remnant of the founding fathers died. Jefferson and John Adams had died just five years earlier, and Madison was still alive and active. One section of Tocqueville's study was entitled "Religion considered as a political institution which powerfully contributes to the maintenance of a democratic republic among the Americans." In this section, and several subsequent ones, he makes some interesting observations.

> It may be asserted, then, that in the United States no religious doctrine displays the slightest hostility to democratic and republican institutions. The clergy of all the different sects there hold the same language; their opinions are in agreement with the laws...

> Religion in America takes no direct part in the government of society, but it must be regarded as the first of their political institutions; for if it does not impart a taste for freedom, it facilitates the use of it.

> ...but I am certain that they hold [religion] to be indispensable to the maintenance of republican institutions. This opinion is not peculiar to a class of citizens or a party, but it belongs to the whole nation and to every rank of society.

> Despotism may govern without faith, but liberty can-

not.... How is it possible that society should escape destruction if the moral tie is not strengthened in proportion as the political tie is relaxed?

Tocqueville wrote his study based on extensive interviews and personal observations of Americans in several states. Tocqueville's principal biographer, the American historian George Pierson, wrote in 1938, "[Tocqueville wondered] what had kept [Americans] orderly and moral?... [W]hat was keeping this untutored, self-governing nation from running amuck?... On examining the code of American society, Tocqueville and Beaumont thought they [had] discovered the spiritual safeguards for which they were seeking in two traditions: the traditions of religion and education." In his interviews, Tocqueville learned that religion had been part of education from the first days of the Pilgrims. A strong belief in the value of a moral education for everyone and an insistence on its importance in the maintenance of the democracy were considered salient features of the "American creed." Religious education is what made America work. Tocqueville attached great importance to the moralizing forces of American society and the influence of religion in every sector. Pierson observes:

> The devout quiet in the churches, the deserted Sunday streets, the religious spirit obvious in the conduct and conversation of their acquaintances, deeply impressed the two friends. When, a month later at Auburn, a Presbyterian minister was to say to Tocqueville, "I don't believe a people can be moral if it isn't religious, I therefore judge the maintenance of the religious spirit one of our greatest political interests," he was to

put into words a truth of which his questioner had already become convinced. "Mama and Bébé seemed to fear that I would fall into irreligious ways," Tocqueville was soon to write his brother. "I assure you we are far from that. Never have I been so conscious of the influence of religion on the morals and the social and political state of a people as since my arrival in America. It is impossible not to recognize here the necessity of this motivator and regulator of human actions...." With the thought of the importance of religion, therefore, Tocqueville and Beaumont rounded out their first general analysis of the United States. Environment and custom, the frontier, the school and the church, these had been the great causative influences in the making of the country.

Tocqueville conducted extensive interviews with a cross section of Americans and kept meticulous notes in his journal. These fascinating glimpses of early nineteenth-century American attitudes did not appear in his book.

*Interview with the Rev. James Richards.*

Religion? I don't believe that a Republic can exist without morals and I do not believe that a people can have morals when it isn't religious. I therefore judge the maintenance of the religious spirit one of our greatest political interests.

*Interview with a Mr. Spencer.*

Q. To what do you attribute the religious tolerance which reigns in the United States?

A. Principally to the extreme division of sects (which is almost without limits). If there were but two religions, we should cut each other's throats. But no sect having the majority, all have need of tolerance.

Moreover, it's a generally accepted opinion, in which I concur, that some sort of religion is necessary to man in society, the more so the freer he is...

Q. Does the clergy direct your public education?

A. Absolutely. I know of only two exceptions in the state of New York. This state of affairs seems to me quite natural.

*Interview with a Catholic priest.*

Q. Do you think that the support of the civil power is useful to religion?

A. I am profoundly convinced that it is harmful. I know that the majority of Catholic priests in Europe have a contrary view ... If they could live in this country, they would not be long in changing their opinions. All religious beliefs are on the same footing here. The government neither sustains nor persecutes any one; and doubtless there is not a country in the world where the Catholic religion counts adherents more fervent and proselytes more numerous. I repeat, the less religion and its ministers are mixed with civil government, the less part will they take in political dissensions, and the more power religious ideas will gain.

*Interview with Louis Dwight.*

Q. Do Americans believe, as do some in Europe that simply by having taught a man to read, write, and count, one has made him a good citizen, and almost a virtuous man?

A. Doubtless not. No one would be found here to sustain the thesis, so often maintained in Europe, that education can have ill effects; but each takes it for granted that the instruction given will be moral

and religious. There would be a general outcry, a
kind of popular uprising against the man who would
introduce the contrary system, and each would be
better than instruction given in that manner...

Pierson summarized the observations in *Democracy in
America* as rooted in three assumptions. For the successful practice of self-government, Tocqueville recommended: (1) religion (i.e., a church separated from the
state and a faith that taught morality and respect for law
and order); (2) experience and practice in self-control;
and (3) the maximum decentralization.

You might wonder what all this history has to teach
us about school prayer in contemporary America. In
England and then in America, the struggle over religious freedom was centered on the government's desire
to control all religious expression, including corporate
prayer. The government, and many of the religious factions that competed with it, wanted to regulate both the
form and content of every public expression of religious faith. People were willing both to die and kill in
the cause of religious conformity. Laissez-faire in religious matters was out of the question. State officials and
church authorities were coconspirators in a policy of
repression that was legally comprehensive, enforced by
the civil courts, carried out by local magistrates and
backed by military power. American colonists continued this policy in Massachusetts and throughout New
England. Today, some people still hold that only one
belief system is worthy of state approval: secularism.
Today's magistrates—jurists and legislators—have con-

structed a legal labyrinth that effectively controls every aspect of religious expression in public schools.

Modern methods of control are far more subtle than those of seventeenth-century England but no less effective. Principals, teachers and students must negotiate a legal thicket of laws, regulations and policies intended to ban all references to religion. The government's reach extends into every corner of the educational system, defining and redefining the limits of permissible expression. The new definition of tolerance is exceedingly narrow and excludes Christian and Jew, Muslim and Buddhist. Indeed, every expression of belief in the sacred is excluded. Is this tolerance?

State-sanctioned bigotry took many forms in England and America but the principle was always the same. Repression was the mathematical constant of intolerance. Whenever the free exercise of religion was stifled, intolerance grew. Yet today, our courts enforce a secular hegemony against all forms of religious expression in our schools. This is based on a new but pervasive assumption, borrowed from the social sciences, that secular education is value free. Under the pretense of loyalty to the First Amendment, the courts have advanced the notion that a secular education implies an absence of values, good or bad. The reasoning goes like this: If you remove religion from schools, a moral vacuum is established. Every student can pass through this vacuum without encountering a single value-charged atom. Therefore, each child will rely on his or her own (individual and family) values.

This theory is based on the naïve belief that all secular disciplines are morally "neutral," "objective" or "scientific." This is a myth. The curricula of our schools are heavily value laden. Unfortunately, those values are not always consonant with the community. Antireligious sentiment is often hidden under a veneer of neutrality. In our schools, secular doctrine now has the force of law. The old tyranny of a state religion has been replaced by the new tyranny of a state secularism. Both are equally distasteful. History teaches us that all repression is hateful.

Many early settlers sought these shores because they did not have the right, among others, to pray according to the dictates of their conscience. The desire to separate church and state was based on Locke's principles and was intended to remove from government the power to control or exclude anyone on the basis of his religious convictions. Yet there was never any intent, any thought, of eliminating religion from public life. The 1962 and 1963 court decisions banning prayer in public schools did not further the cause of church-state separation as it was originally conceived. The Court's decision, whether it intended to or not, contributed instead to a process in which one set of values was increasingly given preference over all others. The fight for religious liberty was motivated by a passionate belief in the importance of religion itself. It was not a fight to establish secularism or to remove every vestige of the sacred from public life. The architects of liberty were themselves religious, deeply so. Their writings do not support an antischool prayer position. There is no basis for such an idea among the principal theorists of religious freedom. They believed unequivocally in the value of religious training for every child. The pervasive secularism that would eventually lead to the banning of school prayer was the result of a long, gradual process that only gained momentum many years later.

We may well ask how did this happen? How did religious freedom turn into religious constraint? The answer to that question is not simple, but this much can be said: It is the consequence of many transformations in which the accomplishments of thinkers like John Locke and Thomas Jefferson were turned upside down. We are the descendants of Enlightenment thinkers who remade the world by giving birth to freedom but who also planted the seeds of other intellectual and social philosophies that became completely secular. The question of whether our children will be able to pray depends, in part, on whether we remember our religious past. The temptation is to succumb to amnesia; to be carried on the tide of indifference.

Ignorance does not indemnify us from the consequences of forgetting this history. If we are to fashion a future for ourselves in which God has a place, we must first know where we have come from. The history of our religious freedoms is as important as that of our family or nation yet too few of us know it. We can neither uphold and honor nor intelligently criticize and change what we do not know. The foundation of democracy is an informed, active citizenry, but too few of us know the history that led to the framing of our Constitution—or how the Supreme Court has changed its meaning in modern times.

The moral instruction envisioned by Locke has been replaced by a secularism hostile to value-based curricula and religious inquiry. Secular education has relegated these issues to the scrap heap. Attempts to subject education to the rigor of a new scientific secularism has produced a generation of children suspicious of moral judgments. This is the dark side of the Enlightenment, which gave us religious liberty but also empowered us to establish a secular society distrustful of religion. Yet in the thinking of Locke, Isaac Newton, Thomas Jefferson and other Enlightenment visionaries, secular knowledge and religious wisdom were equally legitimate pursuits. Scientists and theologians alike engaged in education—neither had a monopoly. Science did not denigrate or seek to avoid questions of religion, and vice versa. There were no disciplinary or legal boundaries between the two. Locke and Jefferson recognized that the world is made up of spiritual as well as physical and material values. In our time, we have separated the sacred so far from our schools that issues of religion have become completely irrelevant to many educators. They can think only in terms of secular goals. We have lost something important.

# Key Court
# Decisions

Public education in America was rooted in religion from the very beginning. Harvard College, founded in 1636, has these words inscribed on the wall by the Johnston Gates:

> After God had carried us safe to New England, and wee had builded our houses, provided necessaries for our liveli-hood, rear'd convenient places for God's worship and setled the Civill Government; One of the next things we longed for, and looked after was to advance Learning and perpetuate it to Posterity; dreading to leave an illiterate Ministery to the Churches, when our present Ministers shall lie in the Dust.

Originally, the school was thought of as an arm of the church and the instruction students received was infused with religious principles. Elementary instruction focused on the three *Rs*, the Bible and the catechism. The *New England Primer,* used from 1700 into the 1850s, taught reading by means of an acrostic in which each letter of the alphabet was illustrated with a religious aphorism. Word lists were always slanted toward a moral purpose, and as students built their vocabulary they began to read with texts such as the Ten Commandments, stories from the Bible and the Westminster Catechism. But the colonies, and later the states, had different approaches to public education. In the south, there was virtually no widespread education until revolutionary times because of the southern colonies' strong links to the Church of England. The liturgical nature of Anglican high church worship made it the least Bible centered of all the Protestant groups. Traditionally, education had been stressed more by Puritans and separatists for whom literacy was important. These groups insisted on the need for their children to read the Bible. This situation changed with the eighteenth-century religious revival known as the Great Awakening. Eventually a push for literacy was made throughout the colonies. In the middle colonies, schools were founded, financed and administered by local churches; teaching certificates were issued by governors and religious groups. The headmaster was typically a clergyman. In the New England states, schools were supported by tax funds collected by colonial magistrates. Teachers were approved by town meetings, selectmen, school committees and ministers.

After the Revolutionary War, schools began to lose their denominational character. They came to be less controlled by sponsoring churches and less sectarian in their curricula. Many of the states had written into their constitutions provisions similar to the First Amendment and consequently state-sponsored church-related schools began to die out. There were so many different religious groups that it became impossible to teach sectarian doctrine without the threat of fragmenting the entire public school system. Local governments willingly filled the gap, becoming increasingly interested in public schools because they believed a healthy democracy required an educated citizenry. As a result, states moved to create a new institutionalized school system sponsored and administered by local boards. In 1785, Congress set aside lot 16 of every new township in the territories for the establishment of public schools. Congress made its intention clear: "Religion, morality, and knowledge being necessary to good government and the happiness of mankind, schools and the means of education shall forever be encouraged." Congress intended the schools to be nonsectarian and free from the doctrinal control of any denomination, but not secular in the sense of the *Murray* v. *Curlett* decision. For most people then, schools existed not only to teach a general curriculum but also to encourage children to become moral citizens. To this end, religious instruction was permitted in the schools. The prevailing sentiment of the eighteenth and nineteenth centuries was reflected in Court decisions.

> ...the Bible, and especially the New Testament [should] be read and taught as a divine revelation in the [school], its general precepts expounded ... and glorious principles of morality inculcated ... Where

can the purest principles of morality be learned so
clearly or so perfectly as from the New Testament?
  —SUPREME COURT, 1844

In general, people believed that the essence of religion
was to be found in its abstract moral principles.
Throughout the eighteenth, nineteenth and into the
twentieth centuries, schools adopted curricula in which
students were taught good citizenship and civic morality. The main concern at that time was to eliminate any
sectarian doctrine. This meant the exclusion of "sectarian particularities," not religion as a whole. Most people
insisted on the necessity of including an emphasis on
those beliefs that every religious person affirmed: the
existence of God and a moral order. Sidney Mead, in
his history of religion in public schools, concluded that
Americans in the absence of an established church
adopted the public school. The schools took over the
function that had always been assigned to state churches
in other countries: making citizens moral.

From 1791, when the Bill of Rights was ratified, until
the midpoint of the twentieth century, few cases relating to the religion clauses of the First Amendment came
before the Supreme Court. Most of the court decisions
about religion were made at the state level. Although
the First Amendment denied the federal government
any power to interfere with religion or to establish religion, similar actions on the part of the state were not
prohibited. As new states applied to Congress for
admission, it insisted on constitutional guarantees of
freedom of religion and separation. Consequently, most
states had bills of rights or state constitutional provi-

sions assuring religious freedom from the very beginning, but these were interpreted variously. State judges did not always apply the law vigorously and because no U.S. constitutional issue was at stake, the Supreme Court stayed out. In 1810, Chief Justice John Marshall, who served under presidents Adams and Jefferson, hinted that the Court might be willing to extend the prohibitions of the Bill of Rights to the states in *Fletcher* v. *Peck.* He said, "The Constitution of the United States contains what may be deemed a Bill of Rights for the people of each state." But in 1833, in *Barron* v. *Baltimore,* he backed away from the idea, saying, "These amendments contain no expression indicating an intention to apply them to the State governments. This Court cannot so apply them." In *Permoli* v. *First Municipality of New Orleans,* eleven years later, the Court reaffirmed its stand, stating that the free exercise clause of the First Amendment did not apply to the states: "The Constitution makes no provision for protecting the citizens of the respective States in their religious liberties; this is left to the State constitutions and laws; nor is there any inhibition imposed by the Constitution... in this respect on the states."

The basis for change was established with the adoption of the Fourteenth Amendment in 1868. This amendment specifically forbids any of the states to "make or enforce any law which shall abridge the privileges or immunities of citizens of the United States" or to "deprive any person of life, liberty, or property, without due process of law." This amendment raised the question, or at least suggested the possibility, that the federal Constitution was thereby "absorbed" by the states. In a sense, the Constitution was nationalized, thus making the Bill of Rights superior to any state law. However, the Supreme Court consistently rejected this idea until 1925. In the landmark *Gitlow* v. *New York* case, Justice Edward T. Sanford opened the door slightly. The *Gitlow* case involved questions of free speech and the press. Justice Sanford said in the Court's decision, "For present purposes we may and do assume that freedom of speech and press—which are protected by the First Amendment from abridgment by Congress—are among the fundamental personal rights and 'liberties' protected by the due process clause of the Fourteenth Amendment from impairment by the states." Fifteen years later, the door would be thrown wide open.

The watershed year was 1940, and in a landmark case, the Court applied the Fourteenth Amendment unambiguously to the states in *Cantwell* v. *Connecticut.* The Court's judgment reversed an earlier Supreme Court decision made in the *Barron* v. *Baltimore* case in 1833. In the 1833 case, Chief Justice Marshall wrote, "These amendments [Bill of Rights] contain no expression indicating an intention to apply them to the State governments. This Court cannot so apply them." Justice Owen J. Roberts, taking a 180-degree turn, declared in the *Cantwell* decision:

> The fundamental concept of liberty embodied in that Amendment [14th] embraces the liberties guaranteed by the First Amendment. The First Amendment declares that Congress shall make no law respecting

an establishment of religion or prohibiting the free exercise thereof. *The Fourteenth Amendment has rendered the legislatures of the States as incompetent as Congress to enact such laws.* The Constitutional inhibition of legislation on the subject of religion has a double aspect. On the one hand, it forestalls compulsion by law of the acceptance of any creed of the practice of any form of worship. Freedom of conscience and freedom to adhere to such religious organization or form of worship as the individual may choose cannot be restricted by law. On the other hand, it safeguards the free exercise of the chosen form of religion. Thus the Amendment embraces two concepts—freedom to believe and freedom to act. The first is absolute but, in the nature of things, the second cannot be.

For the first time in more than 150 years, the Supreme Court both applied the First Amendment to the states and established a definition of what constituted "minimal prohibitions." This was a mixed blessing. It was good in the sense that it extended First Amendment rights to the citizens of states in which recalcitrant legislatures sometimes ignored or restricted the freedoms of their constituents. Our Constitution is, after all, the foundation of American political society. The decision clearly spoke out against the evils of legal compulsion in matters of religion, but it also extended the reach of the federal government into areas that were formerly matters of states' rights. In this sense it consolidated federal power in a way that was unprecedented. This was not the Court's last word on the matter. Justice Hugo Black, building on the *Cantwell* decision in a later case, would extend this definition further. Black wrote in the *Everson* v. *Board of Education* decision:

> The "establishment of religion" clause of the First Amendment means *at least* [emphasis added] this: Neither a state nor the Federal Government can set up a church. Neither can pass laws which aid one religion, *aid all religions* [emphasis added], or prefer one religion over another.... No tax in any amount, large or small, can be levied to support any religious activities or institutions, whatever they may be called, of whatever form they may adopt to teach or practice religion. Neither a state nor the Federal Government can, openly or secretly, participate in the affairs of any religious organizations or groups and vice versa...

This has remained one of the most important decisions regarding the establishment clause in constitutional case law and has been at the heart of every school prayer decision handed down by the Supreme Court. In my own litigation, Justice Clark quoted his colleague Justice Black in the *Everson* decision. Even though *Everson* was a split decision, not a single justice took issue with the concept of "minimal prohibitions." Is this a justifiable legal concept? The claim that government cannot "pass laws which aid one religion, aid all religions, or prefer one religion over another" is dubious. There is little doubt that the founders intended the establishment clause to mean that government cannot "aid one religion" or "prefer one religion over another." There is no evidence, however, that they meant to prohibit the aiding of religion in general. In fact, there is strong evidence to the contrary.

In his book *Separation of Church and State,* Robert Cord writes, "American history, [sic] shows that on a non-discriminatory basis the Catholic Church and Protestant denominations–including church schools–were directly aided by federal money through treaty obligations, federal legislation, and even, in some cases, control of large grants of land to help propagate the Gospel among Indians." Justice Black's claim that the government cannot spend any public money at all on even remotely religious activities does not describe the government today any more than it describes government in the past. Cord writes, "Did not the prayers of Congressional Chaplains in the First Congress, which formed the Establishment Clause, constitute 'religious activities'? Were their salaries not paid from tax revenues? Are not these same activities, performed in the U.S. Congress today, irreconcilable with the Court's interpretation?"

Justice Black's claim is impossible to support historically. Any attempt to use his argument in support of banning prayer is highly problematic. Even if we think our forebears were unwise and prohibit all direct monetary aid to religion, we are still left with the problem of arguing from history that the Constitution intended to prohibit all aid to religion. The founders thought that religion was essential to the survival of democracy. Therefore, they thought the general support of religion a good, even necessary, thing. As long as government encouragement of religion is not coercive to those who opt out of religious life, it is very difficult to argue on constitutional grounds against the general encouragement of religion. Even if it is successfully argued that we should comprehensively oppose all aid to religion, monetary or otherwise, we are still left with a long leap to the conclusion that the simple granting of permission to children to pray is *aid* to religion. Is such a denial neutrality or hostility?

In the early years of this century, religious leaders were concerned that children were not learning the particular contents of their own faith. People harbored a growing fear that American children were becoming religiously illiterate, but also realized there was little the public schools could do about it. They began to look for ways in which schools could cooperate with religious interests to address the problem. In 1914, in Gary, Indiana, an experiment was launched called release time. With the consent of parents, students could be excused for a specified length of time each week to attend churches or synagogues and receive religious instruction. At the end of the designated period, they returned to school and continued their normal curriculum. In 1940, this same type of plan was instituted in Champaign, Illinois, but with one significant difference—religious classes were held in public school buildings. Religious teachers would come into public classrooms and students who desired religious instruction were assigned to religiously homogeneous groups. Students who did not wish to participate were allowed to do some other task or simply studied until the religious classes were over.

Several years after the release plan was instituted, Mrs. Vashti McCollum sued the school district. This case was made possible by the *Cantwell* v. *Connecticut* decision handed down just eight years earlier. McCollum's son was a nonparticipant, and she stated in her complaint that the district's plan was a violation of the establishment clause. The Supreme Court heard the case in the 1948 *McCollum* v. *Board of Education*. Justice Hugo Black wrote the Court's majority opinion, and he argued that release time aided religious groups in spreading their faiths through improper use of public school taxes. Moreover, he said, the state's compulsory school attendance laws enabled teachers of religion to gain a captive audience. He said, "This is not separation of church and state." Remember, the words "separation of church and state" are not in the Constitution. Nevertheless, the practice was ruled unconstitutional.

Four years later, the Court considered a similar case in *Zorach* v. *Clauson*. In this case, the justices reviewed a New York law allowing the release of children who had parental permission to attend religious classes off campus. The only difference between this case and *McCollum* v. *Board of Education* was the location of the instruction. In the majority opinion written by William O. Douglas, the Court upheld the constitutionality of the New York law. In defending their decision, the justices referred to the role religion had always played in the life of America. Douglas argued that by allowing release time the public schools were doing nothing more than adjusting their schedules to accommodate the religious interests of their constituents. Such a plan, he argued, was not a violation of the establishment clause but an affirmation of the best of our national traditions; to do less would constitute hostility to religion. In this case, Justices Hugo Black, Felix Frankfurter and Robert Jackson wrote strong dissenting opinions. They argued that the location of the religious classes was irrelevant. They contended that as long as school was in session, roll was taken and truancy forbidden for non-participants that the district was working to provide a captive audience for the teaching of religion.

In 1962, the first challenge to school prayer was launched with *Engel* v. *Vitale.* This case was concerned with an invocation intended for use in New York State's public schools. The Board of Regents had written a prayer and urged local school districts to have their students recite it at the beginning of each school day. It was part of a program of "moral and spiritual training," ostensibly to combat "communism and juvenile delinquency." The regents knew the prayer could not be sectarian or in any way "denominational." Consequently, they wrote one so bland it became known among some religious leaders as the "to whom it may concern prayer."

> Almighty God, we acknowledge our dependence upon thee, and we beg Thy blessings upon us, our parents, our teachers and our Country.

About 10 percent of the school districts adopted the recommendation, including the New Hyde Park District, the defendant in the case. Hugo Black again wrote for the majority. He argued that the regents' prayer was clearly unconstitutional regardless of the fact it showed no denominational preference or that students had the right to be excused. He claimed it was a clear violation of the establishment clause. In the opinion he said:

> ...we think that the constitutional prohibition against laws respecting an establishment of religion must at least mean that in this country it is not part of the business of government to compose official prayers for any part of a religious program carried on by government.... The New York laws officially prescribing the Regent's prayer are inconsistent both with the purposes of the Establishment Clause and with the Establishment Clause itself.

The *Engel* v. *Vitale* decision was very controversial at the time. Many people protested loudly, saying that God had been taken out of the classroom, that the school system had been totally secularized, even that schools had fallen prey to communism. Senator Sam Ervin of North Carolina said, "I should like to ask whether we would be far wrong in saying that in this decision the Supreme Court has held that God is unconstitutional and for that reason the public school must be segregated against Him?" Cardinal Cushing of Boston said the decision was "fuel for Communist propaganda." Even Episcopal Bishop James Pike, hardly a conservative, said, "[The Court] just deconsecrated the nation." John Bennett, dean of Union Theological Seminary in New York and a respected scholar, reacted to the decision in an editorial in *Christianity and Crisis.* He said:

> If the Court in the name of religious liberty tries to keep a lid on religious expression and teaching both in the public schools and also in connection with experiments that involve cooperation with the public

> schools, it will drive all religious communities to the establishment of parochial schools, much against the will of many, and to the great detriment of the public schools and probably of the quality of education.

Bennett's moderate words spoke for the mainstream, but many were not so reserved. Communism became the whipping boy for many politicians and clergy. This is the context in which my own case was tried and explains, in part, why my classmates associated my protest more with communism than with atheism. At that time, in the midst of the cold war, people feared that Communists were attempting to infiltrate every aspect of American culture. My mother's political associations certainly lent credibility to that perception. In all this uproar, the Supreme Court agreed in 1963 to hear two other cases on this sensitive issue. There were many more potential litigants. The Religious News Service, after the *Vitale* decision, polled several states and concluded, "First samplings of schools in 15 states indicate that they will continue their former practices of prayer and Bible reading without change." The first of these was *Abington Township School District* v. *Schempp*. The Abington school district was one of many in the state of Pennsylvania that complied with a state law requiring that ten verses of the Bible be read every day at the beginning of school. The reading was to be without comment, and students could request to be excused. The second case was mine. The *Schempp* case and mine were decided together. As noted, the Court applied the "secular purpose" test in its decision. Where the justices had held in the *Engel* case that state-written prayers for public school use were unconstitutional, my own case went beyond that to say that any religious recitation, Bible reading or prayer was a violation of the establishment clause. The decision did not address the issue of what schools could teach about religion in non-devotional, nonevangelistic, strictly academic settings.

That issue was considered in a strange case the Court considered two years later in 1965. The case was *Epperson* v. *Arkansas*. It was triggered by a 1928 Arkansas law, still on the books in 1965, that prohibited the teaching of evolution in public schools. The law was similar to the one in Tennessee that resulted in the famous Scopes "monkey" trial in 1925. In the Scopes trial, a high school teacher named John T. Scopes was charged with violating state law by teaching the theory of evolution. The case received worldwide attention as two mighty egos, William Jennings Bryan and Clarence Darrow, argued the case before hordes of journalists. Scopes was convicted and fined one hundred dollars. In 1965, the Little Rock school administration adopted a biology textbook that contained the theory of evolution. A tenth-grade biology teacher at Central High School, Mrs. Susan Epperson, sued the state to solve a dilemma. The school board had adopted the text but the 1928 law still stood. If she used the text she would be guilty of a criminal offense and subject to dismissal.

The case had acquired very little notoriety, but nevertheless worked its way to the Supreme Court. By the time the justices accepted the brief, it was not known whether Mrs. Epperson was still teaching in Little Rock or even if the biology text was still in use (the answer to both questions was no). The justices, ignoring a free speech issue raised in the lower courts, apparently wanted the case so that they could have the opportunity to definitively settle the issues that had been raised in the *McCollum, Engel* and *Schempp* cases, but had varied from slightly in *Zorach* v. *Clauson.* In the *Epperson* decision issued in 1968, the justices reiterated that the public schools must be secular both in their curricula and related programs. Justice Fortas expressed the same naïve optimism we have seen concerning the ability of the Court to enforce neutrality in his decision:

> Government in our democracy, state and national, must be neutral in matters of religious theory, doctrine, and practice. It may not be hostile to any religion or to the advocacy of no-religion; and it may not aid, foster, or promote one religion or religious theory against another or even against the militant opposite. The First Amendment mandates governmental neutrality between religion and religion, and between religion and nonreligion.

The *Epperson* case more or less marked the end of the radical period of change regarding education and religion. In a little more than twenty years, the Court had ambitiously taken upon itself the goal of redefining the role of religion in America. It had stated its intention to establish a benevolent neutrality but had defined that neutrality in terms of secularism. Subsequent cases built on that legacy. Among them are two that merit attention here.

In 1986, the Court accepted *Wallace* v. *Jaffree.* As it became clear to the states that the Court was not inclined to change its rulings banning compulsory or state-drafted prayer, some legislatures began to employ creative strategies. One of these was the "minute of silence." In 1978, the Alabama legislature passed a statute providing for a minute of silent meditation in schools. Later on, the law was revised to add the words "or voluntary prayer." In 1981, a lawsuit was filed challenging the statute, claiming that it violated the establishment clause. In a 6 to 3 decision, the justices overturned the statute. Justice John Paul Stevens wrote in his opinion that Alabama's law intended "to return prayer to the public schools." The Court, therefore, declared the revised law to be unconstitutional. The justices believed the statute characterized prayer as a "favored practice" and consequently a violation of the secular purpose test: "[The statute] was not motivated by any clear secular purpose—indeed, the statute had *no* secular purpose."

The Court's reasoning here is a real stretch. It seems to me that a very hostile reading of the statute is required to characterize it as establishing a "favored" rather than an "allowed" practice. It also seems to distort history in its implication that a favored practice is an establishment clause issue. We know that the founders would not consider it so. But the Court did not directly appeal to the establishment clause; it referred instead to the secular purpose test and only by implication to the Constitution. Of course, the secular purpose test is not found there. Justice Sandra Day O'Connor left open the possibility that a more carefully worded moment-of-silence law *might* be constitutional. The attorney for the state of Alabama reacted to the decision with these words, "... any mention of God or Christ is viewed as challenging the very deification of man and reason under secular humanism."

Almost thirty years to the day after the *Engel* v. *Vitale* case, the Court handed down the *Lee* v. *Weisman* decision. In June 1989, at a graduation ceremony in Providence, Rhode Island, Rabbi Leslie Gutterman was invited to offer an invocation and benediction at a middle school graduation ceremony. Deborah Weisman, age fourteen, was a member of the graduating class. Rabbi Gutterman delivered this invocation:

> God of the Free, Hope of the Brave:
>
> For the legacy of America where diversity is celebrated and the rights of minorities are protected, we thank You. May these young men and women grow up to enrich it.
>
> For the liberty of America, we thank You. May these new graduates grow up to guard it.
>
> For the political process of America in which all its citizens may participate, for its court system where all may seek justice we thank You. May those we honor this morning always turn to it in trust.
>
> For the destiny of America we thank You. May the graduates of Nathan Bishop Middle School so live that they might help to shape it.
>
> May our aspirations for our country and for these young people, who are our hope for the future, be richly fulfilled. Amen.

To avoid offense, Rabbi Gutterman had submitted his prayer in advance, using the guidelines developed by the National Conference of Christians and Jews in its pamphlet *Guidelines for Civic Occasions.* The school district had invited the rabbi specifically in response to the Weismans' complaints about a Baptist preacher at an earlier graduation. Nevertheless, the Weismans sued, seeking an injunction to prevent the rabbi from pronouncing the invocation. The United States District Court denied the motion saying it had inadequate time to consider the matter before the graduation. Later, Daniel Weisman, Deborah's father, submitted an amended petition asking for a permanent injunction. The federal district court granted the petition, holding the invocation to be unconstitutional. The school district appealed the decision to the Supreme Court. The majority opinion, written by Justice Anthony M. Kennedy, upheld the decision. Kennedy, summing up the results of a half-century of Court decisions, said that the practice of allowing an invocation failed the "three-part Establishment Clause test ... as described in our past cases." The Court's departure from the original intent of the First Amendment, which began in 1940, had hardened into dogma. The decision spelled it out plainly:

> ...to satisfy the Establishment Clause test a government practice must (1) reflect a clearly secular purpose; (2) have a primary effect that neither advances or inhibits religion; and (3) avoid excessive government entanglement with religion.

Is this neutrality? Rabbi Gutterman crafted his invocation with care and integrity. How have we come to the place where a few militant secularists can enlist the government in the censorship of any hint of religion in public ceremonies, no matter how sensitively expressed? Even if one finds the rabbi's prayer somehow distasteful, is it illegal? All of these cases show an underlying hostility to religion and a naïve endorsement of secularism. But there is also another important thread running through them: the issue of free speech. George Orwell, the British writer who feared the abuse of government power and the establishment of a servile citizenry, wrote in 1937, "Freedom is the right to tell people what they do not want to hear." In his chilling book *Nineteen Eighty-four* (written a year after *McCollum v. Board of Education*), he wrote about the suppression of political freedom by thought control. Has the Supreme Court stifled free expression by its suppression of religion in the schools? By insulating some students from expressions they may not want to hear, has the government restricted the freedom of the majority of citizens? More chilling, has the government engaged in a form of thought control by allowing the expression of a single viewpoint? Many people think so.

The full text of the First Amendment reads:

> Congress shall make no law respecting an establishment of religion, or prohibiting the free exercise thereof; *or abridging the freedom of speech* [emphasis added], or of the press; or the right of the people peaceably to assemble, and to petition the Government for a redress of grievances.

School prayer is a free speech issue too. If students of their own accord and acting as private citizens choose to use the public forum of the school in which to pray, it can be argued that such speech is protected under the First Amendment. The ever-inconsistent Supreme Court recognizes this right in most other contexts. The Court recently stated:

> Public places are of necessity the locus for discussion of public issues, as well as protest against arbitrary government action. At the heart of our jurisprudence lies the principle that in a free nation citizens must have the right to gather and speak with other persons in public places. The recognition that certain government-owned property is a public forum provides open notice to citizens that their freedoms may be exercised there without fear of a censorial government, adding tangible reinforcement to the idea that we are a free people. *(ISKCON v. Lee, 1992)*

The public schools are, of course, a public forum and, therefore, using the Court's own reasoning, students have the freedom to pray within them. A federal district court recently stated:

> [P]ublic schools are dedicated, in part, to accommodate students during prescribed hours for personal intercommunication. Unless the students' speech is curriculum related, the speech cannot be limited during those hours on the school campus without a strong showing of interference with school activities or with the rights of other students. *(Slotterback v. Interboro School District, 1991)*

Free speech rights are not absolute. In school, teachers need to exercise a degree of control over the speech and actions of their students. Order needs to be maintained in the classroom and students need to stay focused on the curriculum. But the government must show a reasonable justification for the restriction of any type of speech, because schools are public forums that students are *required,* by law, to attend—a provision that greatly strengthens their free speech rights. Furthermore, any prohibitions against speech must be "*content neutral.*" Content-neutral regulations are those that are "justified without reference to the content of regulated speech" (*Virginia State Board of Pharmacy* v. *Virginia Citizens Consumer Council,* 1976). Therefore, a school absolutely cannot ban religious speech *because it is religious.* It could only ban all speech, during a test for example, regardless of content. And the school cannot ban speech even if other students disapprove:

> If school officials were permitted to prohibit expression to which other students objected, absent any further justification, the officials would have a license to prohibit virtually every type of expression. *(Clark* v. *Dallas Independent School District,* 1992*)*

In my own case, the Court argued that it was unconstitutional to coerce a child into saying the Lord's Prayer, or any other prayer, against his or her will. But coercion is a double-edged sword. Our Constitution guarantees us freedom from all kinds of coercion, including the censoring of our speech. Just as we cannot be coerced into praying, so we cannot be coerced into not praying. Each kind of state-enforced coercion is equally distasteful—and unconstitutional. The Supreme Court itself has said:

> In our system, state-operated schools may not be enclaves of totalitarianism. School officials do not possess absolute authority over their students.

Students in schools as well as out of school are "persons" under our Constitution. They are possessed of fundamental rights which the State must respect, just as they themselves must respect their obligations to the State. In our system, students may not be regarded as closed-circuit recipients of only that which the State chooses to communicate. They may not be confined to the expression of those sentiments that are officially approved. In the absence of a specific showing of constitutionally valid reasons to regulate their speech, students are entitled to freedom of expression of their views.

In *Murray* v. *Curlett,* Justice Brennan employed the phrase "using the words of the First Amendment to defeat its very purpose." School prayer is an issue where school administrators and the courts have done just that. By focusing exclusively upon and distorting the establishment clause, we have allowed government to censor our free exercise and free speech rights. This is an intolerable situation, and one that has a long history. We must not forget that those fugitives from religious repression, the Pilgrims, censored speech too.

The Massachusetts Bay Colony banned free speech and press without a second thought. By law, every Quaker book was burned by the public executioner and its owner fined ten pounds per volume. Roger Williams fled to Rhode Island to establish freedom of speech and religion. In 1671, the governor of Virginia thanked God that the state did not have free speech or press because "learning has brought Disobedience and Heresy and Sects into the world and Printing has divulged them and libels against government." The founders rightly opposed any such censorship. But censorship is the same phenomenon whether it is imposed by religious zealots or narrow-minded secularists. The same injustice that was inflicted on religious minorities by state magistrates is now applied to all religious people by the Supreme Court in the name of "secular neutrality." Rather than establish a new openness, as the Court has claimed, this change has only marked the entrenchment and consolidation of a new intolerant secular order. This does indeed use the First Amendment to "defeat its very purpose."

# Contemporary
# Voices

This is an ideological moment in America. This is
healthy because it involves Americans in reviewing
old themes, arguments, documents and principles.

–GEORGE WILL
*The Washington Post,* April 16, 1995

In his book *The Culture of Disbelief,* Stephen Carter
described the feeling that U.S. intellectuals have fos-
tered secularization in every aspect of our life: education, law, politics, entertainment and the arts. Carter
referred to Phong Nguyen, leader of a Vietnamese
Buddhist congregation in Washington, D.C., who is as
worried as any Christian Coalition activist about the
lack of moral education in our schools. Far from being
the exclusive concern of Christian fundamentalists, the
secularization of society is perceived as a threat by religious people from a variety of faiths. The proponents of

secularization and the separation of church and state honestly believe they advance religious toleration, but Phong Nguyen and others see it as the result of intolerance toward religion as a whole. According to Mr. Carter, the impossible hope of secularists is that religion should be strictly private and have no impact on society.

In the early 1980s, then-exiled Russian novelist Alexandr Solzhenitsyn refused to show up in Washington to receive the $170,000 Templeton Foundation Prize given for progress in religion. Instead, he sent a message attacking the Supreme Court's ban on prayer in public schools, saying, "When prayers in school are forbidden even in a free country, it is not much more tolerable than in Communist countries—only in that it lacks the hammering-in of atheism." Czechoslovakia-born Erica Pinder has been in the United States since the mid-1940s, and she has seen God and religion removed from public classrooms around the country. She worries, "Once you give up a freedom, it is gone forever. We take the Bible to countries around the world, but we don't allow it in our own schools. I don't believe the founding fathers called to separate this country from God or to separate our children's education from God." In her East European childhood, Pinder experienced firsthand the effects of state-imposed secularism.

Alvin Horton's recent editorial, "Prayer for the Sandbox," described the deep frustrations of informed and caring citizens: "I'm dismayed at the inability of parents and school officials alike to find a constitutionally legal way for children to affirm their own religious life without detracting from that of others; and I'm outraged that the fear of controversy can so intimidate our school systems that children are left to treat secularism as a religion in itself." His words bring to mind George Washington's: "Reason and experience both forbid us to expect that the national morality can prevail in exclusion of religious principles. Take away religion, and the country will fail." Yet that is precisely what we have done in our schools.

Some people deny there is a problem at all. Applying the no-problem-is-too-big-to-ignore approach, *USA Today*'s editorial of April 27, 1995, claimed there is much ado about nothing. Saying that students are in no way prohibited or discouraged from praying or studying religion in schools, the editorial asserted that such activities are constitutionally protected. They got it half right. A more realistic view is held by Jay Sekulow, chief council of the American Center for Law and Justice. He is often called upon to defend the parents of religious children. His rebuttal to the editorial offers an extensive list of real-life examples of children—and adults—being limited or discouraged precisely for exercising their freedom of religious expression: A child attempting to sing "Jesus Loves Me" in Washington was told by her teacher that songs like that are inappropriate for sharing time and not allowed in school; department of motor vehicles officials in Oregon disallowed a resident's request to have her custom license plate read PRAY; in California, a pastor throwing a birthday party for his wife was prevented from offering an invocation because the event was held in a rented city-owned facility.

James Wall commented in the *Christian Century* that both sides in the school prayer discussion might not have noticed that schools often simply adopt a neutral voice in moral standards rather than provoke the ire of civil libertarians or secularists. But Mr. Wall is among those who assert that religious rights are protected and, therefore, offenses must not be occurring. "The courts have affirmed the right of student religious groups to meet for prayer and Bible study in public schools outside of classroom time. It is in voluntary settings, which are already open to students, as well as in countless congregations and youth groups, that faith can best be shared, enriched and developed. Rather than focus on the empty symbol of school prayer, we ought to do more with the freedom that students already have to express religious concerns..." Leslie Harris, public policy director for People for the American Way, feels that "students are already free to say a prayer silently. I think they want to allow proselytizing in schools and workplaces." Fear of what might happen produces much heat and not much light around this issue and any description of what has already happened is often disregarded.

Other opponents of school prayer include the National Council of Churches, which has argued that children's lives are not transformed by "magical incantations" but by the models set for them in the conduct of their elders. Church-state expert Dean Kelley stated then that "to press prayer into service as a device for improving the moral climate of the schools is to demean it from an *end* in itself (communion with God) into a *means* to another, lesser end: improving the *behavior of other people's children* [emphasis added]." The national PTA position on prayer in public schools admits the value of a religious education, but the PTA feels strongly about the family context for development of religious values. "Recognizing the diversity of beliefs and religious denominations among our nation's families, the responsibility for these matters must rest with the home and family. PTA members should accept the responsibility for the moral and spiritual education of their children and youth, noting that the spiritual strength and moral growth sought for our young people may be achieved through careful precept and example as well as through religious exercises." The American Bar Association's official stance is against officially sanctioned prayers. ABA president Roberta Ramo said legislative reform is a "terrifying step" toward government interference with religion. But N. Lee Cooper, who will assume the ABA presidency in 1996, values "spiritual revival in our communities" and hopes to moderate some of the association's party-line values.

Supporters of voluntary school prayer agree that it should not be a magical incantation or a means to an end in itself. Supporters also agree that the primary responsibility for spiritual development rests with parents and that officially sanctioned prayers are unacceptable. However, the point is elsewhere. Students themselves feel they are being restricted in their religious expression. When polled about the problem of religion in school, Mississippi students replied that not only were constitutional issues at stake, but fundamental cultural values were too. One young woman said that prayer is the answer rather than the problem: Prayer does no harm; it is "the solution to the values problem." In another school, a student described herself as "a citizen of the United States, a future teacher, and a future parent." In an essay on the First Amendment she wrote: "Whether we be Jewish, Muslim, Buddhist, Catholic, Protestant, Mormon, Seventh-Day Adventist, Quaker, Christian Scientist, Mennonite, followers of Reverend Moon, Secular Humanists, or agnostics–all of us believe in either a Supreme Being, Nature, or Ourselves as determinants of our lives' course." Citing a Massachusetts judge, the essay continued, "Providing an opportunity for students to meditate or pray does not advance religion; it allows serious reflection or contemplation on a subject which may be religious, irreligious, or nonreligious." Instead, she said, meditation is effectively an educational goal– it helps encourage students to turn their minds silently toward serious thoughts and values; it helps students to learn a degree of self-discipline. This idea was echoed by members of the Bible club at Minford High School in New York. They agree on the importance of respecting all faiths, and in the controversy over school prayer, they have struggled to hang on to what is important: "[It's] not so much prayer in school, but prayer in students. If we put the prayer back in the student, we'll have schools with higher morals, better discipline."

Those who advocate school prayer recognize and

honor the fact that we live in a pluralistic society. Pluralism in religious expression is synonymous with American values. We may worship differently from our neighbor next door, but by and large, we do worship. And Buddhists, Jews, Christians and Muslims—every faith in our nation—are subject to the repressive effects of the Supreme Court's limitations on religious expression. Within our borders today are more than seven hundred nonconventional religious denominations, notes Richard Ostling in his 1993 book, *One Nation Under Gods.* Our nation encompasses an unprecedented variety of faiths. We are a nation of immigrants and with these immigrants has come a fantastic diversity of religions. As sociologist Wade Clark Roof has observed, pluralism is at the heart of the American experience. We have a long tradition of accommodating religious differences.

Aside from prayer in schools, widely diverse religious groups are finally winning the right of individual expression in limited contexts. The courts have been maddeningly inconsistent regarding religious rights. While they have been more than willing to restrict free speech, recently they have been somewhat more generous in matters of religious dress and other practices. Failing to distinguish between verbal and nonverbal forms of communication, the Court has occasionally allowed customs that convey a religious message but still ban prayer. Muslim women applying for driver's licenses are now allowed by the department of motor vehicles to be photographed with their veils on; prison inmates may appeal to keep their Rastafarian dreadlocks; Baptists and non-Christians alike have kept the state from erecting a statue of Jesus on a state highway; and Atlanta Muslims convinced their employer, the state of Georgia, to allow them to participate in traditional Friday worship. But the courts are capricious in their rulings: They have banned many Santeria rituals; Oregon's National American [Indian] Church was prohibited from using peyote at religious rituals; an air force rabbi could not wear his yarmulke (even though Congress passed head-covering exemptions for Orthodox Jews and Sikhs); imprisoned Muslims in New Jersey could not attend Friday worship.

Surprisingly, the case that aroused the united concern of organizations across the political spectrum, from far right to far left, was the Oregon case. The case was heard by the Supreme Court as *Employment Division* v. *Smith,* in April 1990. The period following the decision in that case, 1990 until 1993, was called the reign of terror. The Court's decision in the matter was very controversial, and it has remained the topic of conversation ever since. It is emblematic of the Court's fickle attitude about religion. Law professor Michael McConnell, writing in the *University of Chicago Law Review,* called the decision "undoubtedly the most important development in the law of religious freedom in decades." Prior to 1990, the Court generally ruled that government had no right to restrict the free exercise of religion in cases where a sincerely held religious belief was involved or where that belief was burdened by some government action. If these two conditions were met, the government had to show a "compelling government interest" before interfering with a person's religious rights. In the absence of a compelling interest, free exercise prevailed, and any government restriction on religious practice was generally rejected.

In *Smith,* the Supreme Court upheld Oregon's denial of unemployment compensation benefits for two Native American church members who had been fired for their sacramental use of peyote. The two men were employed as drug rehabilitation counselors and fired for their religious practice. They had assumed that their ancient ritual was a constitutionally protected religious exercise. Instead of deciding the issues of the case as they were raised and debated through a long process in the lower courts, however, the Supreme Court used it as an opportunity to make a broad statement about the limits of religious freedom.

In its decision, the Court arbitrarily weakened the legal standards that had previously applied to the free exercise clause of the First Amendment and jettisoned the compelling interest doctrine. The Court said, "We cannot afford the luxury of deeming presumptively invalid, as applied to the religious objective, every regulation of conduct that does not protect an interest of the highest order." The decision was characterized by critics as the equivalent of saying the free exercise rights of the past were a "luxury the nation could no longer afford." According to the justices, any law that did not specifically single out religion as its "object of regulation" (as in Oregon's *blanket ban* on the use of peyote) would be held valid, regardless of whether it trampled on ancient religious rights. John Whitehead and James

Knicely, of the Rutherford Institute, wrote of the *Smith* case:

> ...five members of the Court joined a sweeping opinion written by Justice Antonin Scalia and arbitrarily and dramatically emasculated the legal standards that had previously applied to Free Exercise claims. Compared to the First Amendment's doctrinally vigorous and judicially favored Free Speech, Free Press and Establishment Clauses, the already chronically weak Free Exercise Clause was further debilitated by Justice Scalia's opinion.
>
> The problem with the Smith decision is not so much *what* the Court ruled as *how* it reached its result. The Court's deliberate slighting of one of the two express "conscience" clauses in the Constitution is truly amazing, not only for the continued vitality of individual rights under the Bill of Rights, but also as expression of the Court's apparent unconcern for the reasons the framers adopted the Free Exercise Clause. As constitutional attorney William Bentley Ball observed, "[T]he court's opinion is strikingly cold in reference to religion. *The tone is entirely one of limitation and curbing, as though the free exercise of religion is a danger to be closely confined....*"
>
> Traditionally, whenever it has been claimed that a state law of general applicability interferes with religious practice, the Supreme Court has subjected the restriction to careful scrutiny. In recent years, when a law or government action affected rights of conscience, the Court applied the "compelling state interest" test. In order to overcome a religious liberty claim, the state had to prove that its legislation advanced a "compelling state interest...."
>
> The reasoning in *Smith,* in contrast, seriously jeopar-

dizes the pre-*Smith* standards protecting religious liberty. The Supreme Court concluded ... that the traditional "compelling state interest" test need not be employed in the case of so-called "generally applicable" laws regulating socially harmful conduct. Such religiously neutral laws, the Court said, may bypass the test and need only be rationally related to a legitimate state interest.

In reacting to the *Smith* case, Congressman Stephen J. Solarz said in a *Newsday* article:

The implications of this ruling are staggering and extend far beyond the concerns of Native American religions. Minors may no longer be permitted to participate in religious rituals involving wine. Jews and Moslems whose religions mandate ritual slaughter could be unable to obtain religiously sanctioned foods under broadly-written animal welfare legislation. Those religions that require special articles of clothing or strict standards of modesty could be penalized by workplace and schoolhouse dress codes. Even the practice of ritual circumcision could be outlawed if certain elements viewing the procedure as unnecessary prevail on state legislation to ban it.

Solarz turned out to be right. From 1990 to 1993, free exercise rights were under constant attack. A Minnesota court decision supporting the rights of Amish was overturned. Religious rights were lost in cases involving immigration, landmarking, religious clothing, workers' compensation, home education, zoning, jurisdiction of the National Labor Relations Board over religious schools, the applicability of various federal acts over religious organizations and many other cases.

The *Lang* v. *Sturner* case is a perfect example of the consequences of the *Smith* decision. In the *Lang* case, a federal district judge, specifically citing the *Smith* decision with "profound regret," denied the free exercise claims of a Laotian Hmong family. In this case, the county medical examiner had insisted on conducting an autopsy on the Langs' son, even though he had not died of suspicious causes. The Langs had objected, stating that according to the Hmong religion an autopsy was a mutilation of the body. Hmongs believe that if a body is mutilated, the spirit of the person would not be free and would, therefore, return and take another person in the family. The judge reluctantly ruled against them and noted that the "silent tears [of the other Hmongs] shed in the still courtroom as they heard the Langs' testimony provided stark support for the depth of [their] grief."

Because religious freedom was dealt such a devastating blow by the *Smith* decision, a bipartisan effort was launched in Congress to redress the situation. The result was the Religious Freedom Restoration Act. This is the heart of the act:

> In general: Government shall not burden a person's exercise of religion even if the burden results from a rule of general applicability, except as provided [below].

> Government may substantially burden a person's exercise of religion *only* if it demonstrates that application of the burden to the person (1) is in violation of a compelling governmental interest; and (2) is the least restrictive means of furthering that compelling government interest.

The act was passed in late 1993 and restored to American citizens the constitutional standard that had existed prior to the *Smith* decision. What had previously been assumed as a constitutional right is now guaranteed by an act of Congress. This is an inherently weaker right in that it is a matter of statutory law and not part of the Constitution itself. But its passage seems to have changed the tide of religious repression. The government must once again have a compelling reason to deprive citizens of their right to engage in religious practices.

The Supreme Court's attitudes toward religion and religious expression are undertheorized in every area and betray an appallingly shallow understanding of its nature, practice and role in society. There is no single unifying set of principles underlying the courts' decisions except the discredited one of secular neutrality. The incalculable riches of the world's religious traditions are unknown and underappreciated by much of our judiciary. Consequently, there is no widespread recognition of the fact that moral order is necessary to achieve political order and that until a human society can achieve spiritual harmony within itself, it can never obtain political or social harmony. Yet this is the consensus of every ancient religious faith on Earth. It is the basis of Christianity and Judaism, but it is also the tradition of the Koran, the Vedas of the Hindus, the Way of Buddhism, the Analects of Confucianism, and countless other religious traditions. The accumulated wisdom of millennia has been systematically eliminated from our schools and public places. In its place we have substituted a smug scientism, a narrow-minded secularism and a hostility toward religion.

Nevertheless, many supported the *Smith* decision, blind to the implications and inured to the consequences. Sometimes this support came from surprising places. George Will applauded the decision in a *Washington Post* column. He wrote:

> To understand the philosophic pedigree of Scalia's sensible position is to understand the cool realism and secularism of the philosophy that informed the Founders.
>
> A central purpose of America's political arrangements is the subordination of religion to the political order, meaning the primacy of democracy. The Founders, like Locke before them, wished to tame and domesticate religious passions of the sort that convulsed Europe. They aimed to do so not by establishing religion but by establishing a commercial republic—capitalism. They aimed to submerge people's turbulent energies in self-interested pursuit of material comforts.

George Will, who usually gets it right, got it wrong in this case. The founders certainly did not intend to subordinate religion to the political order. In fact, they desired just the opposite. Religion had already been subordinated to the state with disastrous consequences in England and America. And while there were unquestionably commercial interests at work in the American Revolution, it is anachronistic to describe the founders' motives in terms of capitalism. There was no clear concept of capitalism or the mechanisms of the marketplace until after Adam Smith's *The Wealth of Nations* was published in 1776. It could not have contributed to intellectual ferment in the colonies until after the Revolution was over. More likely, if Smith was known to the founders at all when the Constitution was written, he would have been known for his previous work on religion and conscience, *Theory of Moral Sentiments,* published in 1759. Both works reveal Smith's firm belief in the importance of religion. It took many years for Smith's books to be distributed and become part of the intellectual conversation in America. Will, like others, confuses a late twentieth-century concept of secularism with that of Locke and the founders. This confusion has serious consequences. The Supreme Court, attributing an equally anachronistic definition of secularism to the founders, has based a whole doctrine on it. As James Madison said, "There is not a shadow of right in the general [federal] government to intermeddle with religion."

Since Christians form the largest religious group in America, they have borne the brunt of official discrimination. There is reason for Christians to feel that the courts discriminate against them in particular rather than against religious expression in general. For example, at the University of Virginia, a state-funded institution, where cultural diversity is actively pursued, support was denied for a Christian magazine. In spite of claims of political correctness on campus, the university provided publication subsidies for such diverse groups as the Muslim Student Association and the Jewish Law Students Association. Appeals for funding for a Christian publication were denied. In its defense, the university claimed that funding for the other groups was intended to encourage diversity but not the support of religion. In the words of one religious leader, however, there is a nationwide groundswell of insistence on "equal access to the marketplace of ideas." It is pure discrimination, he said, to do less. Ronald Rosenberger, in spearheading efforts to gain university funding for the publication, noted that "we aren't seeking special rights or privileges; we're just seeking equal access." Michael Greve of the Center for Individual Rights observed, "This is viewpoint discrimination, pure and simple."

The overzealous application of the Court's secular neutrality doctrine is widespread. Some of it is the result of fear on the part of school officials. Misunderstanding of the law is common and as a result it is often applied with a rigor that the courts did not intend. Sometimes religious people are persecuted by those who simply resent Christians, Jews or Muslims. People on the fringe who hate religion are part of the picture. My brother, Jon Murray, is president of American Atheists, Inc. According to Jon, there is "no place for [religion] in the marketplace of reasonable ideas or in the public schools of our time." Many secularists embrace this ideological hegemony. They do not want a free expression of ideas in our schools. What is reasonable to them may not be to me. We each have a right to express our own "reasonable" beliefs in the marketplace of ideas. University officials are not quite so crass as my brother, but sometimes they too share a basic mistrust of religion and religious people. This is prejudice, plain and simple.

Sometimes an action is the result of ignorance, but at other times, it is ill will. At a high school in Wynne, Arkansas, administrators banned the distribution of religious materials on campus. Attorneys pointed out that the school could not do so unless it banned the distribution of all materials, and if it banned all materials, it must do so in a way that did not impinge on the First Amendment free speech rights of students. The school backed down. In Kalamazoo, Michigan, Eric Pensinger sued his high school to have a portrait of Jesus removed from a hallway. A federal court ordered its removal, and the Supreme Court declined to review the matter. The portrait, which had hung for more than thirty years, "advanced religion," according to Judge Gilbert S. Merritt, by virtue of its "proselytizing" effect. Another judge countered that the famous portrait "no more conveys the notion of 'establishment' than a statue of Robert E. Lee in a park suggests we should dissolve the Union." Nevertheless, the order stood. Subsequently, the plaintiff's lawyer refused to accept the grouping of the picture with portraits of Gandhi, Martin Luther King, Jr. and Abraham Lincoln. This lawyer treated the portrait as if it were pornography. And Judge Merritt's reasoning almost implied that it had magical powers to convert students—by merely looking at it!

In West Virginia, a school denied a junior high Bible club permission to take a field trip to Washington, at its own expense, to attend the National Day of Prayer. Previously, the school had granted permission to the cartoon club, computer club, ski club, drama club and several other clubs to go on field trips during school hours. The district had provided buses and teacher chaperones for some of them. The only club denied permission was the Bible club. The school even announced its intention to penalize those who went on the trip with an unexcused absence. A federal judge finally ruled that the school district was being prejudicial in its policy. Instances like this illustrate how the Supreme Court's decisions have institutionalized a deep distrust of religion in our schools.

In March 1995, religious leaders from organizations as diverse as People for the American Way and the Christian Coalition met to discuss their differences. When they finished, many disagreements remained, but on several key points they had found consensus. They published a statement entitled "Religious Liberty, Public Education and the Future of American Democracy." In it they agreed on five important points: (1) Religious liberty is the right of every person. (2) Citizenship means respecting difference. (3) Parents are responsible for the religious education of children. (4) Schools must model the democratic process. (5) Civil debate is at the heart of a true democracy. With this hopeful conclusion, the groups returned to their own agendas, vowing to keep the fight civil. If the University of Virginia had embraced these tenets, perhaps a more open-minded policy might have resulted.

Also in March 1995, *60 Minutes'* Lesley Stahl presented a segment on Lisa Herdahl, a resident of Pontotoc County, Mississippi. Many of Mississippi's public schools still include devotions and prayer. As the local folk describe it, "It's their way of life and not to be denied." Ms. Herdahl sued the county school district, asserting that organized prayer in school is unconstitutional. Her children were raised as Lutherans, and she herself was raised in the Christian Science tradition. Nevertheless, her children chose to walk out of their class's devotion, and reported feeling discriminated against by their peers as a result. A federal judge in the case struck down most of the county's law authorizing student-led prayer, exempting only prayer at high school graduations. He said, "Even though the prayers are student-led, students who did not want to hear them or participate would still be coerced to take part in a 'captive audience' situation." School superintendent Jerry Horton said in the school's defense that the situation "was solvable" and no one's rights were being violated: "It's controlled by the students. It's student-initiated. We feel like it's protected by the Free Exercise clause of the First Amendment." Speaking on behalf of the Herdahls, People for the American Way expressed concern about the supportability of claims made by religiously homogeneous communities; if the Herdahl family did not wish to participate, they should not have to conform to local practices or leave town for a more religiously tolerant community.

This case raises all the important issues. Is student-initiated, student-led prayer, as Jerry Horton called it, the equivalent of an "establishment of religion"? Is the Herdahl children's discomfort a relevant legal issue? How are the rights of the majority and minority balanced? Is the community being deprived of its right to the free exercise of its religion? What about the free speech issues? Where is the locus of authority? If a school district makes reasonable provision for dissent and nonparticipation, are anyone's rights being violated? What is to prevent the tyranny of the minority?

Jeremy Rabkin, associate professor of government at Cornell University, has taken a long view of judicial action since 1940. "The Supreme Court has used the supposed menace of religion in public schools as a doctrinal and political launching pad for broader attacks on religious references or accommodations to religion in public life. Some justices have even argued, in so many words, that the Constitution requires religious opinion not only to be hidden, but also to be disenfranchised." Mr. Rabkin puts religious influence in schools into perspective: "The truth is that while schools may usually try to avoid giving offense, no one seriously pretends that schools have a constitutional duty—or even a practical hope—of making every student feel equally comfortable at all times." School sporting contests and patriotic rituals exemplify areas of student involvement from which some students will be excluded. "It may not always be possible to satisfy everyone. After all, the issue is not really one of assuring accommodation of differing viewpoints and trying to limit wounded feelings." The issue is essentially one of assuring that the public schools remain committed to a policy of "approved" secular neutrality.

The school prayer rulings have been called whimsical by conservatives, a mere "policy preference on the part of 20th-century liberals," disguised as "Constitutional fundamentalism." In a December 1994 *Time* magazine essay, "Let Us Pray," Richard Brookhiser described an underlying fear of being influenced by each other's religion as equal to people's distrust of atheists. Harking back to the Constitution's original wording, the author located the concept of inalienable rights in the notion of a creator. Those rights are our divine endowment; the laws of nature, and nature's God, depend on a theocentric worldview. Brookhiser parsed nature into two categories: history (as nature in time) and will (as nature in us). Implied in both is an active God. His essay presents two interesting conclusions: Our rights are best preserved when we see them as derived from a fearsome source outside ourselves, and society should know the source of those things it holds dear. He notes that this complex issue is attributed with creating many strange alliances, citing the subject as being more popular than discussions of homosexuality. And he wryly notes it's the only area capable of uniting the politically disparate voices of Newt Gingrich and Marion Barry. In the American south, Brookhiser says, both whites and African Americans jointly protested the firing of school principal Bishop Knox over his decision to allow prayer at a school event.

Amid the wide variety of opinions in the public forum, a clear majority of Americans favor the return of voluntary school prayer. By mid-1994, at least twelve states had, or were about to enact, laws approving student-led prayers. In early 1995, a *Washington Post*/ABC poll concluded that of the several mandates we have

given our elected leaders, prayer in school rated sixth
and stood as the lone moral issue driven by constitutionality. Of those polled, some form of school prayer is
supported by 67 percent. A review of public opinion
over the past three decades shows a distinct curve
toward, then away from, opposition to school prayer. In
July 1962, a Gallup poll indicated that 85 percent
favored approving religious observances in schools. By
1980, only 55 percent were in favor of required prayer,
according to Gallup. Sixty-nine percent were in favor of
voluntary prayer in a *Time* magazine poll the following
year. But ten years later, 78 percent of those polled by
*Time*/CNN supported the right of students to pray in
public schools. While a poll is by definition a general-
ization of opinion, the numbers consistently indicate
throughout this thirty-year span that a significant plu-
rality of Americans favor some form of meditation or
prayer in school—whether voluntary or mandated, quiet
or spoken. In his 1994 national research survey *Virtual
America,* demographer George Barna observed that
"many leaders might be surprised by some of the
choices people would lean toward. For instance, the
matter of school prayer is not much of a struggle for
most people. Nearly 9 out of 10 adults aged 18–98
(85%–87%) said they would favor allowing prayer in
public schools, as long as it is done on a voluntary
basis." In comparison with another of Mr. Barna's subject areas, within the same sample group, only 49
percent would favor restricting distribution of porno-
graphic material.

What's been going on in our world to bring us to this

point? David Barton listed several key events in his 1988 book, *America: To Pray or Not to Pray*. The 1950s marked the Korean War and the beginnings of desegregation; the 1960s saw school prayer being removed, the civil rights and voting rights movements, the heating up of American involvement in Vietnam, protests against the war, the assassinations of President Kennedy, Martin Luther King, Jr., and Robert Kennedy and desegregation of schools. In the 1970s, school busing was controversial, and our last official combat troops left Vietnam. Mr. Barton's book includes extensive research into American behavior in the years following 1962 in the categories of students, their parents and families, academic leaders and the nation. His graphs illustrate that measurable positive behavior declined and corresponded with the 1962 and 1963 Supreme Court decisions that removed prayer from schools.

Sociologist Robert Bellah has studied the relationship between Americans and spirituality in their public and private lives. Using the term "civil religion," he has described the connections between religious faith and our democratic values. More than a dozen years ago, he voiced the fear that our nation's highly valued individual autonomy had been seriously eroded. Dr. Bellah interviewed Americans on the subject of their freedom not to have other people's values, ideas or lifestyles forced upon them. His research showed that our so-called secular freedom tends to undermine human commitment and yields a bottom-line mentality that says "you're responsible for yourself and no one else."

Says Dr. Bellah, "If I am responsible for myself alone, then my feelings, wishes and desires are the only ultimate criteria, standard or norm for my actions. Thus all unsatisfying relationships are dispensable, the individual is absolute, and ultimately we are our own god. In such a world, there is room only for a purely privatized faith that only serves the function of therapy for private individuals. In this world, the therapist and manager, both understood to be neutral and value-free, replace the priest and the politician, both of whom represent an outside moral vision oppressive to the radical individualist."

Contemporary Americans live in tension between the desire to express their deeply held religious convictions and the fear of becoming subject to someone else's faith or ideology. This widespread cultural anxiety is reflected in contemporary court decisions that treat religion as inherently dangerous. The clear message of the courts is that religious faith is volatile and potentially explosive. The smugness of court decisions through the 1960s and 1970s suggested that religion was an outdated cultural artifact possessing sentimental value but of limited utility in the modern world. But now religion is viewed by some as a threat to democracy. As Americans have witnessed the rise of Islamic fundamentalism and warring factions divided along religious lines in Eastern Europe, faith has often been equated with fanaticism. Consequently, Americans have been willing to exchange limitations on their religious freedoms for the implied security of a secular neutrality. But this is a hopelessly naïve exchange.

There is no security in state-enforced secularism, as the collapse of communism has amply demonstrated.

The collapse of communism was as much the result of a crisis of spirit and human values as economics. Any state-enforced hegemony of ideas is inherently dangerous. Contemporary Americans no longer fear the threat of communism; they fear the encroachment of their own government. This fear is expressed by critics of every political stripe. On the far left, current thought is obsessed with the "deconstruction" and "decentering" of authority (Derrida, et al.). On the far right, volunteer state militias are equally obsessed with conspiracy theories of government. The vast middle is just confused. Secular neutrality has not delivered the goods. Our schools are not better off for it.

# Education
# in Crisis

Our public schools are in trouble. The reasons for public education's decline are complex, but the warning signs are clear and compelling. Our youths are in distress. The statistics documenting the full extent of the situation fill whole volumes, but it is worth reviewing a few of them here. William Bennett, the former secretary of education, published a study entitled *The Index of Leading Cultural Indicators*. In it he made the following observations:

- ◆ In the 1988 International Assessment of Educational Progress exams in science, U.S. students scored last among tested nations.

- ◆ Since 1965, the juvenile arrest rate for violent crimes has tripled.

- ◆ The fastest growing segment of the criminal population is our nation's children.

◆ Twenty percent of high school students now carry a firearm, knife, razor, club or some other weapon on a regular basis.

◆ In 1990, more than two thirds of all births to teens were to unmarried girls, compared to less than one third in 1970.

◆ Births to unmarried teenagers has almost doubled since 1960.

◆ Since 1960, the suicide rate among teenagers has more than tripled. Suicide is the number-two killer of adolescents.

Regarding academic performance, the 1983 National Commission Report, *A Nation at Risk,* concluded: "If an unfriendly foreign power had attempted to impose on America the mediocre educational performance that exists today, we might well have viewed it as an act of war." But the problem transcends academic performance. As the statistics show, many young students are in a severe moral crisis, either abusing themselves or those around them. Perhaps the most telling of Bennett's charts is the list of the top seven disciplinary problems in schools, according to public school teachers in 1940 and in 1990.

| *1940* | *1990* |
|---|---|
| Talking out of turn | Drug abuse |
| Chewing gum | Alcohol abuse |
| Making noise | Pregnancy |
| Running in the halls | Suicide |
| Cutting in line | Rape |
| Dress-code violations | Robbery |
| Littering | Assault |

No one doubts that our nation's children are in trouble. The evidence is so overwhelming that to deny it is impossible for all but the most resolutely self-deluded. The decrease in intellectual capital, the increase in major crime and violence, the decrease in responsible sexual choices, the prevalence of drugs and suicide—these trends should be a clarion call to our society. Our children are morally adrift, and they are despairing. The problem is at its worst in our inner cities, where it is deeply bound up with broken families and welfare dependence. The burdens some schools have been forced to bear cannot be overestimated. They have had to feed the hungry, tend the wounded, counsel the distraught, police the delinquent. As Dr. Diane Ravitch, professor of education at Columbia University, has said, "[Modern schools] are so overburdened with responsibilities of many kinds, that somehow their basic responsibility for education has been overwhelmed by all of these other needs." The schools have, in too many cases, been forced to act as parent. Bennett writes in *The De-Valuing of America:*

> [A]s the teachers tell us, more and more parents dropped their children at the doorstep of the school and were gone to pursue their own interests.

The architects of public education never intended the schools to shoulder all these responsibilities. The situation within the public school system has become so chaotic that many concerned parents have abandoned them. There has been a steady stream of students entering private schools since 1960. Without these students, who come from predominately middle-class parents, public education will continue to decline.

Many parents have removed their children from public schools to avoid the prevailing theories and attitudes of many educational theorists, administrators and teachers toward *values*. Many others have been seduced by an insidious moral relativism disguised as an objective and balanced moral neutrality. Moral relativism grows directly out of a secular worldview. It was inevitable that relativism would become the pervasive morality in school because when religion and the values that come from religion were removed, a vacuum was created that had to be filled by something. No environment is free of values. This is as true in matters of morality as it is in physics: Nature abhors a vacuum. With religion gone and secularism in its place, schools have inevitably embraced moral relativism. Moral relativism and secularism go hand in hand; neither has anything positive to say about values. Values are a fundamentally sacred concern.

Most public schools have adopted a vision of "secular neutrality that closely resembles the Supreme Court's. Like the courts, schools must recognize secular neutrality for what it is—a distinct, identifiable value system. School prayer, which represents a sacred and moral worldview, has been pushed aside and replaced by an aggressively secular ideology. If we can admit this as a nation and explode the myth of neutrality, we will open up space for competing values, including religion. There is good reason to introduce the sacred back into schools. Given the current diagnosis of our nation's educational system, is it wise to continue our policy of banning the sacred from schools? School prayer is not a panacea for our social ills.

The removal of prayer from schools in 1963 is only one symptom of our national disease. The decline in education is a complex phenomenon and should be treated as such. But I will say this: *Prayer is a cultural marker.* It is indicative of issues much larger than itself. The removal of prayer from public schools is one facet among many of the pervading secularism of our culture. Is the fact that basic civic morality has taken a precipitous decline in the last thirty years merely coincidental? I want to be careful here–I do not want to propose an overly simplistic view of the problems we face. I do want to suggest the possibility that the reintroduction of a sacred perspective in education may help begin to alleviate our moral crisis. To make my case, I want to offer some evidence that our children are, in many cases, definitely *not* being raised in a value-neutral environment.

If some schools are overburdened to the point where they cannot teach our children the ethics of character, as I think they should, they ought at the very least to heed the ancient injunction "do no harm." Unfortunately, in many cases, schools *have* done harm by systematically undermining the moral training parents have given their children. This is a serious claim, and I do not think that in most cases teachers mean ill; the problem has its roots in a deeply flawed tenet of modern educational philosophy.

Many leaders in the educational establishment have

concluded that in our diverse society ethical consensus is impossible. The claim is that because *some* moral decisions are debatable, controversial and exceedingly hard to make, then *all* of morality must be that way. Because sincere, well-meaning Americans disagree on difficult issues such as war, abortion or affirmative action, they have concluded that morality must always be relative and subject to opinion, and therefore the upholding of any standards would be arbitrary and unfair. As William Bennett writes in *Our Children and Our Country:*

> [D]espite the beliefs of the majority of Americans, no sooner does anyone begin to point out how important it is to "teach values" in the schools than others immediately begin to raise the specter of awful complexity. As soon as someone starts talking about forming character at school, others claim that it just can't be done, that we won't find a consensus on what to teach or how to teach it.

And so they argue in circles. Ultimately, paralyzed by complexity and doubt, educators have embraced an intractable moral relativism. This position, like many extreme and unreasonable positions, has its origins in a moderate and reasonable observation: Ethics are complicated, and loyalties can come into conflict. People with integrity *do* sometimes have different ethical opinions, but does this undermine the whole concept of ethics? Of course not. The problem is that much of the educational establishment has fallen into the trap of casuistry.

"Casuistry" is a term used in ethics and theology to

describe the exploration of the "hard cases," the circumstances where there is a conflict of duties. Casuistry is a practice that challenges all the general rules with particular exceptions or with fundamentally unresolvable paradoxes. For example, a casuist may ask how we are to decide who dies on a sinking ship with a limited number of lifeboats. This is the kind of question that cannot be decided satisfactorily, but it does not therefore render all questions of ethics similarly unresolvable. Or again, to the statement "One should strive to be honest," the casuist may respond, "Honest in telling the ax murderer where he can find your best friend?"

Just because we have found a conflict of duty where honesty is less important than care for others, the principle of honesty has not been undermined! No purpose is served by presenting a child with a complicated, far-fetched hypothetical situation—one that will never be encountered in real life. Because some people might place more emphasis on justice than compassion, it does not follow that either concept is bankrupt. Casuistry is a very limited practice and is not an appropriate activity to engage in with children. Children need to know how to be good people. Former generations knew it was far better to give examples of honesty and heroism. Aristotle was one of the original ethical theorists, and he had little regard for those who simply argued about morality without doing good. Philosophy, he thought, was of no use if it did not lead one to becoming a better person. In the *Nicomachean Ethics,* his main treatise on morality, Aristotle wrote:

The many, however, do not do [moral] actions but

take refuge in arguments, thinking that they are doing philosophy, and that this is the way to become excellent people. In this they are like a sick person who listens attentively to the doctor, but acts on none of his instructions. Such a course of treatment will not improve the state of his body, any more than will the many's way of doing philosophy improve the state of their souls.

At some point the arguments must stop so we can acknowledge our common ground. We must teach what we *do* have in common to our children. But making such a move is not possible when we approach values from a secular perspective. Moral relativism does not provide a rudder to steer through moral waters. But it is not impossible to decide on common values. Ethics are not so complicated that we cannot hold up certain standards of conduct as good, desirable or moral. This is the common sense of the matter. Ethics cannot be approached as problems of logic, and it is useless to judge all of morality on the hard cases.

If we stop arguing in circles and assess those traits we consider admirable in a people, we will find at the end of the day there is considerable agreement about fundamentals. We would be hard pressed, for example, to find people who disagree about the desirability of values such as honesty, integrity, loyalty, fairness, altruism, justice, compassion. Everyone wants his children to express these and other positive character traits, even if there is sometimes disagreement about how to apply them in particular circumstances. Nevertheless, some educators have judged all of morality on the hard cases and refuse to acknowledge that any actions are necessarily better than others; in other words, they have become complete relativists. This is the secular trap.

Relativism would be less troublesome if it was what it pretended to be: neutral. The idea that relativism is value free, however, is a useless fiction; relativism is decidedly value laden. Unfortunately, educators, endorsing the idea that it *is* neutral, have turned relativism into an institutionalized ethic—one that is *taught.* Rather than simply giving up on morality altogether, leaving such matters to parents, many schools actively support moral relativism. This has taken shape during the past two decades in values clarification curricula. In these classes students are encouraged to develop their own morality, without the guidance of parents or teachers. As Bennett writes:

> Starting in the early seventies, "values clarification" programs started turning up in schools all over America. According to this philosophy, the schools were not to take part in their time-honored task of transmitting sound moral values; rather, they were to allow the child to "clarify" his own values (which adults, including parents, had no "right" to criticize). The "values clarification" movement didn't clarify values, it clarified wants and desires. This form of moral relativism said, in effect, that no set of values was right or wrong; everybody had an equal right to his own values; and all values were subjective, relative, personal. This destructive view took hold with a vengeance.

The relativism taught in such classes sometimes reached ridiculous heights. The initially admirable goal

of building a level of flexibility and toleration of differences into moral decision making was extended to
absurdity. Bennett is fond of quoting an anecdote he
read in a 1985 *New York Times* article. Bennett writes:

> In the course of [a high school counseling] session the
> students concluded that a fellow student had been
> foolish to return $1,000 she found in a purse at
> school. According to the article, when the students
> asked the counselor's opinion, "He told them he
> believed the girl had done the right thing, but that, of
> course, he would try not to force his values on them.
> 'If I come from the position of what is right and what
> is wrong,' he explained, 'then I'm not their coun-
> selor.'"

Once upon a time, a counselor offered counsel...

This radically nonjudgmental neutral academic
approach to ethics is totally out of place in a classroom
of young students. When our children are young we
should not ask *them* what morality is; instead, we should
be teaching them by word and example how to be
good. It is a myth that classes like the one Bennett
describes *don't* teach children values. They do.
Educators think that this supposedly hands-off attitude
creates a harmless moral environment, a vacuum
through which students pass untouched by any value
system. The idea is absurdly naïve. *Relativism is a moral
position just like any other.* This is a particularly salient
point for proponents of school prayer. Prayer was outlawed because it is religious and explicitly value laden.
But secular moral relativism is no different. Relativism
is not neutral; it is a value system in itself and it is a fun-

damental mistake to uncritically embrace it as value free while banning religious activities for being value laden.

It might be said that a nonjudgmental attitude is "somewhat" value laden but nevertheless the "most balanced" option available because it takes the "most passive, least aggressive stance toward values." But this claim fails on two counts. First, relativism is not passively but *actively* encouraged. Second, even if relativism was only passively encouraged in schools, the idea that being nonjudgmental is the most balanced and nonaggressive approach falls apart under close scrutiny. By far the most balanced approach is to encourage, in broad terms, the formation of universally agreed upon, positive character traits.

It is understandable why educators would try to be as nonjudgmental as possible. Unfortunately, some classes go much further than simply subscribing to the naïve but well-intentioned moral vacuum theory. Many schools actually *teach* moral relativism—sometimes practically enforcing it—by explicitly privileging it over the morals taught by parents. Relativism has been written right into the curriculum.

Thomas Sowell, a senior fellow at the Hoover Institution and author of *Inside American Education,* researched classes where old values were systematically questioned and a supposed value neutrality was established in its place. His thesis is that schools have become more and more politicized and that solid educational subjects and critical thinking have correspondingly suffered. In the place of solid subjects, the schools have increased electives and substituted values clarification, sexual education, death education, nuclear education, quest, drug prevention, decision making and a whole myriad of other programs instead. The purpose of these classes is not to foster the critical thinking skills demanded of a democratic citizen, but to indoctrinate children with particular social or political views. Their titles make them look very different, but they all have much in common. They frequently work at cross-purposes with parents' views and morals. Sowell writes:

> So-called "sex education" courses and textbooks, for example, seldom involve a mere conveying of biological or medical information. Far more often, the primary thrust is toward a *re-shaping of attitudes,* not only toward sex but also toward parents, toward society, and toward life. The same pattern is found in many other programs claiming to be about drug prevention, smoking prevention, or many other worthy purposes.

The fact that these classes are not what they appear to be is in itself a cause for worry, but far more disturbing is the fact that these classes aggressively target children's values and attempt to replace them with a relativistic moral neutrality. They do so by explicitly engaging and challenging the values the child has adopted from his or her parents, church and society at large. The most common assumption in these programs is that decisions are *not* to be made by relying on traditional values passed on by parents. Instead, parental values are to be questioned and compared with the values of other individuals or other societies. This is to be done in a neutral or nonjudgmental manner, which does not seek to deter-mine a "right" or "wrong" way but what feels best to the particular students. This approach is called values clar-ification. Its focus is on the feelings of the student rather than on the requirements of a democratic society.

These values clarification classes are certainly not neutral. It is interesting that they conceal themselves behind very misleading labels. As Sowell notes, values clarification classes hardly clarify anything. Instead, they often leave the child deeply confused about what, exactly, is right and wrong. Rather than give children a healthy sense of the diversity of their peers, which I imagine was the original purpose, it makes them ques-tion the whole moral enterprise. According to Sowell, "The very phrase 'values clarification' is fundamentally dishonest." When parents teach their children not to steal or not to have sex, there is no ambiguity of mean-ing. *Clarification is neither required nor attempted.* In many schools, values are treated as the "subjective prefer-ences" of individuals or "our society" and contrasted with alternative values of other individuals and other societies. The nonjudgmental approach of such exer-cises provides no principle of morality from which to choose among the alternatives presented—except what "experts" or "modern thinking" might prefer. "Clari-fication" is merely a word used to hide a process of undermining the child's existing values.

Although this strikes many parents as an act of war, I would like to think that these programs are more mis-guided than willfully harmful. Nevertheless, it is impor-tant to recognize these educators' flawed secular assumptions. The anger of parents is not misplaced, especially in light of the techniques used to instill moral relativism. They are manipulative and high pressure. Sowell has gone so far as to dub them "brainwashing" classes, drawing parallels to the techniques used in Maoist China.

> Instead of educating the intellect, these special curriculum programs condition the emotions. This is sometimes called "affective education," as distinguished from intellectual education. It can also be called brainwashing.

That is a very serious charge, but Sowell backs it up with evidence. He documents how these programs use classic brainwashing techniques such as emotional stress, desensitization, isolation, cross-examining, stripping defenses and rewarding acceptance of new attitudes. Emotional stress can often be generated through sexually explicit, violent or otherwise disturbing movies, props or materials. Techniques are brought to bear through the highly manipulated use of social pressure, such as singling students out for ridicule or having a particular student's beliefs "voted upon" by the class. It is beyond the scope of this book to deny or substantiate Sowell's claim of brainwashing. But I do want to affirm his assertion that the principles by which our children learn to judge morality have been left to "what peers or 'experts' or 'modern thinking' might prefer." The folly of leaving children to guide other children's moral development hardly needs comment; this is the blind leading the blind. The idea that children should rely on modern thinking is merely another way of saying they should rely on secularism for moral guidance. Secularism has nothing useful to say about morality and ultimately leads to relativism. The idea that children should turn to the "experts" for moral guidance is absurd, but increasingly they have done exactly that.

By "experts" I mean educational theorists whose ideas get passed down and disseminated through the public school hierarchy. There are three points to make about experts: (1) They are largely secularists; (2) their claims to expertise need to be examined critically; and (3) we have ceded too much authority to them. These theorists have declared themselves "experts" in the field of education, and we have allowed them access into every part of our children's belief system. This is understandable in one sense—people frequently lay claim to more authority than they should. What is not understandable, as Sowell notes, is "why parents and the public allow themselves to be intimidated by such educators' pretensions of 'expertise.'"

The rise of the unassailable expert in a variety of fields, including education, is a relatively recent phenomenon and closely parallels the rise of a secular worldview in America. This is no accident. Our culture's unassailable "high priest" is now the scientist, and anyone who acts from within the boundaries of the scientific establishment commands authority. Therefore, when an educational theorist makes claims about the proper way to educate children, presenting "scientific" data to back those claims, they carry weight. My target here is not science; it is how people make claims of authority. When theorists seize power over our children, we have the right and responsibility to challenge that authority. That authority has important implications for parents who want to see religion on an equal footing with secular ideology. We must hold our educational leaders responsible, and they in turn must defend their belief system with more than a simple reference to prevailing educational theory.

The need to challenge the experts is important; many are using their authority inappropriately. For example, Sowell mentions an episode taken from the book *Child Abuse in the Classroom,* where a parent in Kansas testified about a movie shown to a sixth-grade class:

> The first three minutes of the footage was the actual birth of a baby. It started out with a lady with her legs up and apart, and her feet in stirrups or something like that, with a doctor. It was very graphic and very detailed. The children in the 6th grade witnessed three actual births. I sensed a state of shock in the little boys and girls that it was all new to see a man doing what a doctor does to deliver a baby.

In North Carolina, a child fainted when shown a childbirth movie. In a Kansas classroom, when a parent asked the nurse why they showed the movie in a "health" class, the reply was, "Well, someday they need to learn about these things." Sowell asks the question: "What gave her the right to usurp the decision as to *when* that 'someday' was, and to make it the same day for all children, regardless of their individual emotional development? Clearly," he continued, "she must have realized that it was a usurpation, for the movie was billed as a film on *vitamins!*" Indeed, two thirds of the movie was on vitamins, though the parent who watched it "did not see any correlation between the live births and the vitamins."

My point is not that showing the birth movie per se was inappropriate—although no doubt it was. My point is that we have ceded authority to an educational establishment whose values all too often do not reflect our own and who, despite their claims, are not acting "neutrally." The issue is *who decides* how our children are to be raised. That decision is now centralized and uniform. Jefferson's vision of local control has been lost to a national secular educational agenda, and so has his vision of moral education. So what should we do? I have three recommendations. First, we should acknowledge that as a society we share a great many values in common. We should return to teaching those common values to our children. Second, we must decentralize educational authority and return control to the local level. Third, we should level the playing field and allow the sacred back into the schools so it can, at the very least, compete with secularism and relativism on equal footing.

It might properly be asked whether my optimism regarding the existence of commonly held values is misplaced. I don't think so. C. S. Lewis wrote in *Mere Christianity* how definitions of good and admirable behavior are universal:

> I know that some people say the idea of a Law of Nature or decent behavior known to all men is unsound, because different civilizations ... have had

quite different moralities. But this is not true.... If anyone will take the trouble to compare the moral teaching of, say, the ancient Egyptians, Babylonians, Hindus, Chinese, Greeks, and Romans, what will really strike him will be how very alike they are to each other and to our own.... Think of a country where people were admired for running away in battle, or where a man felt proud of doublecrossing all the people who had been kindest to him. You might as well try to imagine a country where two and two made five.

Moral values across religious and ethnic lines have a great deal in common. That is why I think that teaching character ethics is more balanced than taking a radically nonjudgmental relativist stance toward morality. It is true that we could not spell out an *exact* definition of ethics–and few but a handful of Kant scholars try–but this does not undermine the whole moral enterprise. As Aristotle wrote, "It is the mark of an educated man to look for precision in each class of things just so far as the nature of the subject admits: it is evidently equally foolish to accept probable reasoning from a mathematician and to demand from a rhetorician demonstrative proofs." The point, of course, is that our lack of precision in ethics is to be expected. The living of a moral life more closely resembles art than math. We must not underestimate the importance of agreeing on a core morality, at least in rough outline, because relativism when taken to its logical conclusion leads down a very dark road, one we must avoid. Agreeing on moral standards of conduct gives the counselor in New York permission to say that not stealing a thousand dollars is better than stealing it. It provides moral leverage. C. S. Lewis puts the point very starkly: It is the values we declare universal that allow us to deny that Nazism is simply a choice, no better or worse than any other.

More than simply avoiding the negative consequences of relativism, advocating moral values has demonstrably positive results. One need only look at the difference in national test scores between private religious institutions and public schools. Religious schools, on the whole, test far better than their public counterparts. Gerald Grant, professor of education and sociology at Syracuse University, wrote a chapter in the book *Challenge to American Schools* entitled "Schools That Make an Imprint: Creating a Strong Positive Ethos." The results of his team's research indicate that schools which have explicit character ideals, where the faculty encourages students to become compassionate and fair, do far better than those which do not. In other words, those schools that are unafraid to say what constitutes an excellent person do better both in academics and discipline. Grant observes that the "critical problem for public school leadership is to regenerate a dialogue about the nature of moral community in the school—to recreate a sense of the public good for which public education exists." He identified what many others have recognized is a deep need in modern public education.

The National Commission has recognized public education's loss of direction: "Secondary school curricula have been homogenized, diluted, and diffused to the point that they no longer have a central purpose." We need to renew public education's purpose as a democratic and moral enterprise, and this may only be possible through a renewal of the historical and sacred purposes for which schools were created. This notion is gaining momentum; William Bennett advocates a refocusing of the public school curriculum and a return to the teaching of character. His *Book of Virtues* is one contribution to the cause. I add my own voice, and hope that you will join us. Together, we can turn the tide against the domination of secularism.

We need to transfer control to local authorities. Once there is local control again, we can reclaim "values" classes and make room for competing nonsecular activities in schools. Take these issues from the experts and the courts and give them back to the people. We need a level playing field that allows room for the sacred. Of course, I do not mean that we should institutionalize religion. I do not support any plan that implies the coercion of anyone's conscience. I mean simply that we should allow voluntary corporate prayer in local communities that desire it. We should disestablish secularism as our state religion. To do this would be in harmony with our country's history and one step toward addressing the moral aimlessness of our age. Otherwise the public education system in America is doomed. The brightest, the best, the sons and daughters of the new management class will move totally to private education. This will ultimately lead to a two-tier educational system in America and create an atmosphere in which there is increasing tension between classes and races. No one should be denied a good and moral education because of race or class. Yet in America today, superior education and values are taught in religious and other private schools that are beyond the reach of most citizens.

# Putting It Right

To borrow a line from the Bard, "I am a kind of burr; I shall stick." And so it was with my mother. A chance encounter at Woodbourne Junior High, a stubborn disposition, a propitious time; this powerful synergy eliminated prayer from public schools. My mother, like a prickly burr, stuck to her agenda and pursued her anger all the way to the Supreme Court. It is one of history's ironies that momentous events grow out of spontaneous, unplanned circumstances. My mother had not planned to confront the school counselor. Neither had she given much thought to prayer in schools. She had produced no position papers or scholarly treatises on the subject. It was simply a matter of spontaneous combustion. The accumulated anger of years found focus in a single cause that would change the life of millions of students. The removal of prayer from schools has now been defended by a thousand writers. It has become institutionalized through the courts, rationalized by educational theorists, eulogized by secularists, analyzed by the press and anathematized by conservatives.

Although my mother lit the fire, others had provided the kindling and fuel. It would be a mistake to give her full credit for eliminating school prayer. The process of secularization had been under way for many years. I do not think she had much awareness of that. But she nevertheless launched her attack at a time in which there was a receptive judiciary. And in spite of widespread protests, the time was ripe in the general culture as well. Congress did not succeed in passing a constitutional amendment after the decision, although there was much talk of it. Politicians created a lot of heat but not much light. Americans did not exert sufficient pressure to bring about a restoration either, even though many spoke out against the Court's decision with outrage.

Deep down, underneath the rhetoric, many Americans were conflicted. In their public life they were mostly traditional: churchgoing, family centered, conservative. But on the inside, decades of scientific skepticism had taken root. Schools and colleges had been uncritically advocating a radically secular world-view for a long time. While the critique of secularism was confined to a few intellectuals, a whole generation of GI Bill students were exposed to secular assumptions in colleges and universities. The moral implications of secularism had not been widely explored. Teacher-training colleges, in particular, pumped out thousands of new graduates who received their credentials with little or no background in ethics or moral development. The precepts of behaviorist psychology replaced the moral concepts of religion. Many teachers embraced this new ideology uncritically.

As Jean-François Lyotard said, "If we accept the notion that there is an established body of knowledge, the question of its transmission, from a pragmatic point of view, can be subdivided into a series of questions: Who transmits learning? What is transmitted? To whom? Through what medium? In what form? With what effect? A university policy is formed by a coherent set of answers to these questions."

America was of two minds. On the one hand, the nation was still deeply religious. On the other, skepticism had taken hold. Secretly, many Americans—especially college graduates—harbored the feeling that secularism just might work; that it really was neutral. But this was a false hope. The secular values teachers learned in college and then transmitted to their students failed. In a single generation, the public school system nearly collapsed. Was it a failure of methodology? Perhaps. Were there other social factors as work? Yes. Was it a failure of spirit? Absolutely. The "established body of knowledge" transmitted to students was sanitized of all religious content. With hindsight, we can see the defect clearly. The transformation of education into a secular scientific enterprise has been a disaster.

The 1963 Supreme Court did not exist in splendid isolation. It would be a mistake to confuse the insular nature of the Court with any concept of sociocultural isolation. The justices were insular only in the political/judicial sense implied by their lifetime appointments. The secular myth they transformed into legal precedent reflected an ideology that had been gathering adherents and political power for a long time. Their faith in secularism was only an extension of prevailing intellectual sentiment. They were men of their time. They were lawyers with a legal education. Yet they were called upon to make judgments that impinged on deep matters of philosophy, history and social theory. Our age has been described as one of "epistemological uncertainty." In laymen's terms, this means that people are struggling to find some basis for organizing their lives and finding meaning in them. The 1963 Court showed little sign of uncertainty about anything. It was convinced of the objectivity and neutrality of secularism. The justices had a deep faith in it but that faith turned out to be misplaced. The house of secularism was built on a foundation of sand, and today's intellectual currents have washed it away.

We must constantly remind ourselves that the Supreme Court is a fallible human institution. It is our responsibility as citizens to judge the judges. If the Court strays too far from the Constitution, if it engages in social policy making that is contrary to our national tradition, if it subverts legislative intent, then we must work within our democratic system to bring about change. The Constitution is not carved in stone; it is a fluid and changing document. Americans over the years have modified, extended and changed it twenty-seven times—as recently as 1992. If the Court has improperly established secularism as the new state religion, then we have both the right and the legal means to disestablish it. The Constitution itself provides a mechanism to accomplish this.

The religious freedoms institutionalized in our Constitution are the result of a comprehensible historical process. The justices referred to that history in their defense of secularism but the facts simply do not support the thesis that our founders ever intended to drive religion from civic life. The struggle for religious freedom was exactly that: freedom *for* religion, not freedom *from* it. The assertion that the founders intended to establish a secular state is wholly unsupportable by the historical record. The secularism of the Enlightenment was synonymous with toleration and religious freedom. It was intended to bring relief from state terrorism and government authority over religion. It certainly was not intended to bring about state censorship of religious expression. The names of Locke, Jefferson and Madison, invoked by the justices in their decisions, did nothing to support their cause. None of these historic figures lends any credibility to the Court's position on prayer. Even the most superficial examination of Locke and Jefferson makes any antiprayer position problematic. In the judicial equivalent of psychological projection, the Court read its own position into the historical record. The Court's exegesis is fundamentally flawed.

For centuries thousands of people died in Europe and America in the cause of religious liberty. It is a supreme irony that the freedoms sought by innumerable martyrs, and achieved in our Constitution, were restricted in the name of secularism. The Court subverted religious liberty by an appeal to the literature of religious freedom itself. By the use of two logical fallacies it established a position at odds with history: (1) By *ad vercundium* arguments appealing to our awe for the founders they sought to achieve acceptance of their decision, even though the writings of the founders contradicted it, and (2) by non sequitur reasoning they attempted to establish that our constitutional guarantees of religious liberty were meant to exclude religion! These distortions of common sense are as old as Aristotle's *Sophistical Refutations* and as new as yesterday's Court decisions. What is surprising is that a learned Court would employ such shoddy arguments.

There can be no doubt that John Locke and Thomas Jefferson believed in the importance of religious and moral training in schools. As Jefferson wrote, "All men shall be free to profess, and by argument maintain, their opinions in matters of religion and [government] shall in no wise diminish, enlarge or affect their civil capacities." Today, any attempt to "profess, and by argument maintain" religion in public schools has been deemed unconstitutional. If school is not an appropriate forum for discussing opinions about religion, what is? Locke's belief in the relationship of private morality and public behavior has been lost too. Much less have we considered his stress on the importance of a religious education to the state; and God forbid we should heed his admonition that teachers should instruct students how to pray! In the Court's superficial reading of history, the most disturbing matter is its utter lack of appreciation for the role of religion in a democracy. For Jefferson, the "moral precepts" were indispensable to every person's "social being." Today, the relationship of morality to citizenship has been reduced to a meaningless relativism in which nothing can be unequivocally affirmed. Morality is a strictly private affair and inappropriate in the public forum. Yet learned opinion from Aristotle to Jefferson contradicts this opinion. Indeed, the founders believed that as political bounds are relaxed, morality must be strengthened.

Recent Court decisions have gone well beyond privileging secularism; they suggest an actual hostility toward religion. The source of this hostility is hard to divine. Whether it results from some deep, hidden current in the American psyche, the personal prejudices of the justices or contemporary intellectual fashion depends on whom you ask. The first possibility seems impossible in light of opinion polls about prayer in schools. American public sentiment is overwhelmingly in favor of prayer. The personal psyches of the justices are an imponderable. Intellectual fashion is suspicious of religion, and sometimes openly hostile. Perhaps the wise course is not to formulate explanations but to focus on solutions. The Court's hostility is inappropriate and unfaithful to our constitutional heritage. If our First Amendment rights have become unclear to a myopic Court, then we have the right to clarify them in terms that are completely unambiguous. It is one thing to privilege religion; it is quite another to stigmatize it. Religious viewpoints are entitled to compete in the open marketplace without prejudice or hostility.

With hindsight we can now see that the secularization of our schools has done great harm. No one can claim any longer that change is not needed. During 1994 and 1995, I began working intensively with a bipartisan coalition to restore our First Amendment rights and put religion on equal footing with secularism. After many months of work and input from a variety of sources, several draft constitutional amendments were written. Representative Ernest Istook, with the support of House Speaker Newt Gingrich, will introduce a final draft of the amendment to Congress in 1995.

There are several important observations that need to be made about a proposed amendment. Michael Whitehead, writing in the Southern Baptist newsletter *Salt* (Vol. 4, No. 5, 1994) has summarized the most important points. First, it cannot mandate prayer in schools, but permits it if students choose to initiate it and the school district accommodates it. School prayer was mandatory in Baltimore when I was a student. I am not advocating a return to mandatory prayer. I think any kind of coercion is wrong. As a child, I was caught between the atheism my mother enforced at home and the religion enforced in my school. No child should be subject to these kinds of pressures, and none of the proposed amendments will do that.

Second, the amendment should be framed in terms of a limitation on government power, primarily the federal government. The U.S. Constitution could no longer be used by the Supreme Court, or other courts, to prohibit prayer by private citizens. Students and local school boards would have the right not to have classroom prayer based on local or state decisions, but officials could not appeal to First Amendment or federal court decisions to support the ban. Conversely, districts that choose to allow voluntary prayer would be free of federal interference.

Third, the proposed amendment should not reverse the Supreme Court's decision in my 1963 case, banning government-mandated prayer and Bible reading. Most Americans, including Christians, do not want government dictating religious exercises of any kind. The amendment does not support state-sponsored religion but rejects the idea that a "wall of separation" should be erected that equates separation of church and state with separation of religious speech from public life.

Fourth, the amendment should assume that the government does not necessarily sponsor or endorse everything it allows. Schools and judges often mistake accommodation for endorsement. The idea that student-led prayer is inherently coercive is wrong. As Justice O'Connor has said, there is a crucial difference between *government* speech endorsing religion and *private* speech endorsing religion, which the free speech and free exercise clauses protect. Schools and judges have had a hard time understanding this distinction. A clear statement of student's rights to religious expression is necessary to dispel the de facto hostility that has developed toward religion in public schools.

Fifth, it should not be a "moment of silence" amendment. The Constitution already protects our right to engage in silent prayer anywhere. The proposed amendment should protect the right of prayer and religious expression out loud, so long as it is not disruptive of the school program. The amendment should permit a local board to adopt a moment of silence policy while others might institute a voluntary program of oral prayer.

Sixth, the amendment should seek to restore lost rights. The intent of the amendment is to reinstate and protect the liberty of America's public school students to initiate or lead in prayer or other religious expressions. The amendment does not tinker with the Constitution, but honors the intent of the founders.

Reactions to the proposed amendment have been many and varied. Steven T. McFarland, writing in *Christianity Today* (January 9, 1995), said:

> So what should a constitutional amendment look like? It should primarily be a restoration (rather than a modification) of First Amendment law. The Free Speech and Free Exercise of Religion clauses, as currently interpreted, already provide some protection for student religious expression in public schools. Yet school officials sometimes conclude that the Establishment Clause "trumps" those other freedoms and legitimizes suppression of religious speech. Any proposal should address this bankrupt analysis and educate school officials about what the Establishment Clause actually permits and protects.

Many people have stated that an amendment is not necessary. Barry Lynn, in the *Congressional Digest* (January 1995), argued that prayer is a strictly private affair; consequently, there can be no law prohibiting it. However, Barry's article misses the point: Prayer is equally a social act and exists for the community as well as the individual. Congress opens with prayer on a daily basis; it is a communal gesture. Senator Mark Hatfield argues the same line, saying that prayer is a personal right and no one can stop a person from praying silently, thus no action should be taken to change the law. Both Lynn and Hatfield show little appreciation for the complexity and history of the school prayer issue. Other politicians argue that Congress is wasting its time on "unimportant issues" like school prayer. They fail to understand that the school prayer issue is about fundamental First Amendment rights. William F. Buckley, Jr., writing in the *National Review* (December 1994), said, "'Let's attend first,' Dole is understood to be saying, to 'important things like crime and welfare.' This is another way of saying, 'Let's leave the prayer business for a rainy day.' Which means, 'Let's forget it'—because there is never a rainy day in Congress."

Arthur J. Kropp and David Ramage argue in the *Congressional Digest* (December 1995) that the amendment would set a "dangerous precedent," tampering with fundamental liberties established by the founders in the Bill of Rights. But the proposed amendment does not do any such thing. The First Amendment has *already* been tampered with by the Supreme Court. The goal of the amendment is to restore and clarify its original meaning. The intent of the founders and the decisions of the Supreme Court since 1940 are in clear conflict. It is the Court that has reinterpreted the First Amendment in terms of twentieth-century concepts of secular neutrality. The only "dangerous precedent" at stake is the Court's precedent.

Other critics of the proposed amendment argue that

it violates the concept of separation. Marvin E. Frankel, in the *New Leader* (December 19, 1994), writes:

> The wall of separation has been a treasure for the polyglot American family. The opponents of the principle–those who seek the clout of government to back their religious beliefs–base themselves upon error of history and of true religious devotion. In a long, prudent perspective, it can be seen that they risk freedom of religion for themselves as well as others. The Establishment Clause, properly understood and followed, is a miraculous spiritual boon for America. We should cherish and preserve it.

Frankel misses the mark on almost every point. Proponents of the amendment do *not* seek the clout of government to back their religious beliefs. On the contrary, they want government out of the business of privileging *any* belief system. And "error of history"? Exactly what error does Mr. Frankel have in mind? History completely undermines the position that religion should be excluded from public schools–or any other aspect of civic life. The writings of the founders speak for themselves. Any reading that excludes religion requires a sleight-of-hand exegesis or deliberate distortion.

As we have seen, the Jeffersonian phrase "wall of separation" is routinely misappropriated and used out of context. A "long, prudent perspective" shows a clear trend away from the original intent of the founders. The establishment clause, "properly understood," lends no support to the banishment of religion. Only the most deliberate act of denial can support the notion that the Court's position of secular neutrality has been a "miraculous spiritual boon for America." One wonders if Mr.

Frankel has been in a public school recently, especially in one of the inner cities. Yet this fiction persists, even within the ranks of evangelicals. Forest Montgomery, quoted in a *Christianity Today* article, warned against violating the wall of separation by getting "Caesar in the prayer business." Unfortunately, Caesar is already in the prayer business. We need to get him out.

Perhaps the most persistent argument employed against a constitutional amendment is the fear that it will institute a regime of coercion. This is the issue raised by President Clinton. His initial reaction to a proposed school prayer amendment was "I have always thought that the question was when does voluntary prayer really become coercive to people who have different religious views from those who are in the majority.... I'll be glad to discuss it with them. I want to see what the details are. I certainly wouldn't rule it out; it depends on what it says." A reasonable answer, but under pressure he soon retracted the statement. Making a 180-degree turn, he called any such amendment "inherently coercive." His first response was far more balanced—it really *does* depend on what it says, and the proposed drafts as worded are *not* inherently coercive.

Roger K. Newman, writing in the *National Law Journal* (January 23, 1995), argued that because children are so susceptible to peer pressure, no school prayer could really be voluntary. Joe Loconte, writing in *Policy Review* (Winter, 1995), espouses the same viewpoint:

Some school prayer opponents point to the acutely

peer-conscious climate of the classroom. With organized prayer, students would be asked either to
acknowledge or ignore what is essentially an act of
worship among the faithful. It is one thing for members of Congress to begin a legislative session with
prayer or for the Supreme Court to open with "God
save the United States and this honorable court." But
it's quite another thing for a minor, who has no
choice but to be in school, who is there without her
parents, who perhaps already is having trouble fit-
ting in.

It *is* possible that some children might feel discomfort
during school prayer. It would be unfortunate if students and teachers were insensitive to this issue. Every
student, to the extent possible, should be made to feel
welcome and comfortable in our schools. But schools
cannot ensure the comfort of every student in every cir-
cumstance of their educational experience. Some students feel discomfort because they cannot pray, carry a
Bible to school or speak openly about their religious
convictions. The issue of school prayer exists in a context of competing values. Student discomfort or the fear
of peer pressure is not necessarily more important than
other issues. There are matters of free speech and prevailing community values to consider. Students would
not necessarily be asked to "acknowledge or ignore"
the practice of voluntary prayer. Nonparticipating students, by the very act of nonparticipation, affirm their
constitutional right to be different. This is the essence of
toleration. Toleration assumes difference; there is no
toleration in the absence of conviction.

Not every student believes the same thing. The differences between students should enrich the educational experience. Abstention need not mark students for ridicule. Nonparticipating students create the opportunity for the discussion of different religious or nonreligious viewpoints. This is healthy—mindless, uncritical conformity is not the point. The point is that religious convictions of any kind are now excluded. The amendment does not establish a national standard for schools. Local school districts would be empowered to work out their own solutions. Homogeneous communities may have programs that are quite different from heterogeneous communities. There is no obligation on the part of any school district to do *anything* under any of the amendments now proposed. It would be up to the community.

Peter J. Riga, in the *National Law Journal* (December 12, 1994), expressed his fear that prayer in public schools would divide our increasingly multicultural nation. According to Riga, all of the ethnic and religious strife in the world should teach Americans not to introduce that sort of strife in their own nation. A constitutional amendment would "divide our society" and render the First Amendment "no longer effective" as the "instrument of peace" the founders intended. Joe Loconte harbors the same concern. "A majority-prayer rationale also fails to face the profound cultural and religious diversity that characterizes national life. There are at least 1,200 organized, distinct religious groups in America, many of them outside the Judeo-Christian tradition; self-proclaimed secularists make up perhaps 10 percent of the population, with growing numbers of

Muslims, Hindus, and New Age adherents. Public schools are increasingly becoming flashpoints for such diversity."

My response to Mr. Riga and Mr. Loconte is simple. If a school district feels that a program of voluntary prayer would introduce strife into the classroom, *it is under no obligation to do so.* And who would be in a better position to know than the local community? Every one of the proposed amendments imposes a restriction on the federal government, not local schools. Communities would be empowered to exercise their own best judgment. It is a simple tradeoff: federal power for local control. What's the problem?

Some critics of an amendment suggest that it would institute a tyranny of the majority over the rights of the minority. Of course, minority viewpoints must be protected, but not to the point of discrimination against the majority. Every citizen has basic rights that are inviolable. Any hint of coercion would be wrong. But this is a religious freedoms amendment. It does not provide any mechanism for coercion; it *prevents* the federal government from coercing schools into a uniform secularism—or religious doctrine. I was the only student at Woodbourne Junior High who objected to prayer and Bible reading, yet the entire school was made to conform to my wishes. The principle can be taken too far; the minority can hold the majority hostage. William F. Buckley made this trenchant observation in the *National Review* (December 31, 1994): "[T]he best lesson to teach the idiosyncratic minority is that the majority had certain rights, and even as Public School 81 has the right to assemble a cheering squad to exult over the school's basketball team, the majority should have the right to say something pleasant to God when school assembles in the morning."

The issue for many religious people is whether or not they have the right to control education in their own communities. Bobby Clanton, a school prayer activist from Mississippi, argues that the majority of students in his state are conservative Christians and they should have the right to decide whether and how to pray in public schools. In a *New York Times* article he said, "We're tired of yielding to a tiny minority." Richard Land, a Southern Baptist, says, "Religious expression and dominance in culture must be from the bottom up, not the top down and even then there must be extreme sensitivity on the part of the dominant majority that they don't trample the rights of religious minorities." When authority is from the bottom up, there are built-in forces that help discourage coercion. School policies are able to reflect more accurately the religious or non-religious character of their communities. It is extremely unlikely, for example, that Mississippi and California would have similar policies regarding prayer; an Amish community in Lancaster County, Pennsylvania, would have schools much different from Santa Fe, New Mexico, or Brooklyn, New York.

Implied in the critique of school prayer, among a few evangelicals, is the feeling that prayer must conform to a particular doctrinal standard–their standard–or there should be no prayer at all. "The same parents who press for prayer in the South would be outraged by

Buddhist meditation in Hawaii or readings from the Book of Mormon in Utah," according to Os Guinness, an evangelical writer/commentator. In my opinion, Guinness has misread the situation. If parents in Mississippi had the right to set standards in their own community, most of them would be glad that other communities had the same right. They are smart enough to understand that freedom is reciprocal. Joe Loconte in his *Policy Review* article summed up this fear, "... faith is the most intimate of matters, concerned not with personal preference but with the moral dictates of conscience. And the consciences of society's most vulnerable members—its children—require special protection, particularly in a setting as volatile and influential as public education." The implication is that children must be protected from ill-conceived or unwanted religious expressions. But are children's consciences being protected now? Is a "doctrinally incorrect" prayer worse than the moral relativism taught in most public schools? If public education is truly "influential," what kind of influences are at work now?

Loconte suggests that there are only two ways that school prayer supporters can hope to avoid offending the consciences of various faith communities: Compose prayers so innocuous and devoid of theology that no one could possibly be offended, or allow everyone equal time. The first alternative, he says, results in "a gray, soul-less, generally accepted prayer [that] could not possibly admit most of the divine attributes considered basic to Jewish and Christian believers." Mark Noll, a professor at Wheaton College, agrees, saying, "I don't know how a generic, civil, utilitarian prayer is able to not offend anybody who's serious about his own faith. If you get something that would not offend, then it has to be offensive." "For Christians who take their faith seriously, such a lowest-common-denominator deity is too vague to be useful, too broad to be anything but misleading," says Os Guinness in *The American Hour: A Time of Reckoning and the Once and Future Role of Faith.* Perhaps. But Americans should have the right to express "gray, soul-less" prayers if that is what they choose.

The dismal picture portrayed by these descriptions is very unlikely to happen. A constitutional amendment merely opens the door to experimentation. Michael McConnell, a law professor at the University of Chicago and an evangelical, in commenting on the possibility of school prayer said, "It [could send] the message that one prayer is as good as another. That's simply another way of reinforcing—on a grand public scale—cultural and religious relativism." What these people seem to be saying is that they are offended in advance: No prayer could satisfy them but their own. "If I can't have my prayer, neither can anybody else." And does Mr. McConnell really think that relativism is not *already* being taught? As to the "equal time" alternative, it seems likely to me that highly pluralistic communities would elect to have no voluntary program at all—as would be their right under the proposed amendment.

Loconte also objects to school prayer on the basis that it implies a state endorsement of religion:

...if "student-led" prayers become a routine part of

public education, they could revive a mutated version of civil religion in the schools. Many evangelicals view civil religion as a threat to religious freedom, because in its worst forms it allows the government to establish its own brand of "orthodox" religion, by which it judges other expressions of faith.

There would be no uniform civil religion if the federal government has no control over religious expression in schools. First Amendment guarantees are not compromised; they are strengthened. Local control establishes policy making at the district level. Without an amendment, the federal government will maintain its existing ideological hegemony over schools. We already have the equivalent of an "orthodox" state religion. The religious freedoms amendment takes into account the legitimate fears of Americans. It establishes no form of religion. On the contrary, it protects all of us, religious and nonreligious.

I understand the concern of Americans who fear government involvement in religion. I have been involved with this issue all my life, from both ends of the ideological spectrum. As a teenager, I shared my mother's loathing of religion. As an adult, I came to understand the vital role of religion in the life of this nation. I abandoned my atheism for a life of faith. I was not mature enough in 1963 to perceive the comprehensive nature of the changes taking place in our nation. I did not realize that Mother was just a foot soldier in the war between the secular and the sacred. I knew of her involvement with communism and her deep personal anger but I did not recognize the larger social forces at work. The world is different now. Communism is dead, but secularism is vital and alive. It was easy to focus on communism as a threat. Its rhetoric was front-page news. Secularism is much more subtle and hidden yet secularism was at the heart of the moral crisis that destroyed communism from the inside out. Is our democratic capitalism immune to the same disease? Can our schools survive their own moral crisis?

> There is a tide in the affairs of men
> Which taken at the flood leads on to fortune;
> Omitted, all the voyage of their life
> Is bound in shallows and in miseries.
> On such a full sea are we now afloat,
> And we must take the current when it serves,
> Or lose our ventures.
> —WILLIAM SHAKESPEARE
> *Julius Caesar,* IV:iii:217–23

The tide is changing. In a few years we will enter a new millennium. We will cross a temporal and symbolic divide. It is time for our nation to reevaluate its worldview: its basic values, social and political structures, arts, institutions and public education system. Our time has been called the postmodern age. Nothing "post" is permanent or even long-lived. Ours is a transition period. What America will look like depends on how we respond to the challenges of this current transformation. Our intellectual leaders, business leaders, political leaders, but above all our educational leaders, must return to the wisdom of the past.

Unlike in England, Germany or Japan, in America

we do not have a common heritage. We are many different colors, nationalities and ethnic backgrounds. What will bind us together if not a common belief in God? If we abandon our religious heritage, as my mother and others desire, what will be the bond that holds our nation together? The common thread that binds us as a people is the belief that we are indeed one nation under God. Belief in God is the safety net of our democracy, without which we will surely perish.

[ B I B L I O G R A P H Y ]

*All excerpts and quotations can be found in the sources listed here.*

Ackrill, J.L., ed. *A New Aristotle Reader.* Princeton, NJ: Princeton University Press, 1987.

Alley, Robert S. *School Prayer: The Court, the Congress, and the First Amendment.* Buffalo, NY: Prometheus Books, 1994.

———, ed. *James Madison on Religious Liberty.* Buffalo, NY: Prometheus Books, 1985.

Axtell, James L. *The Educational Writings of John Locke.* Cambridge, England: Cambridge University Press, 1968.

Bennett, William J. *The Index of Leading Cultural Indicators: Facts and Figures on the State of American Society.* New York: Touchstone, 1994.

———. *The De-Valuing of America: The Fight for Our Culture and Our Children.* New York: Touchstone, 1992.

———. *Our Children and Our Country: Improving America's Schools and Affirming the Common Culture.* New York: Simon & Schuster, 1988.

Bunzel, John H., ed. *Challenge to American Schools: The Case for Standards and Values.* New York: Oxford University Press, 1985.

Carmody, Denise L., and John T. Carmody. *The Republic of Many Mansions: Foundations of American Religious Thought.* New York: Paragon House, 1990.

Commission of the Bicentennial of the United States Constitution. *The Supreme Court of the United States: Its Beginnings and Its Justices 1790–1991.* 1992.

Cord, Robert L. *Separation of Church and State: Historical Fact and Current Fiction.* New York: Lambeth Press, 1982.

Cotton, John. "The Bloudy Tenet, Washed, and made white with the bloud of the Lambe..." Photocopy of original, 1647.

Foucault, Michel. *The Order of Things: An Archaeologie of the Human Sciences.* R. D. Laing, ed. New York: Vantage Books, 1973.

Frady, Marshall, ed. *To Save Our Schools, to Save Our Children: The Approaching Crisis in America's Public Schools.* Far Hills, NJ: New Horizon Press, 1985.

Harkness, Georgia E. *The Modern Rival of Christian Faith: An Analysis of Secularism.* Nashville, TN: Abingdon-Cokesbury Press, 1952.

Harvey, David. *The Condition of Postmodernity: An Enquiry into the Origins of Cultural Change.* Cambridge and Oxford, England: Blackwell Publishers, 1993.

Healey, Robert M. *Jefferson on Religion in Public Education.* New Haven, CT: Yale University Press, 1962.

Johnson, Alvin W., and Frank H. Yost. *Separation of Church and State in the United States.* New York: Greenwood Press, 1969.

Konvitz, Milton R. *Religious Liberty and Conscience: A Constitutional Inquiry.* New York: Viking Press, 1968.

Lewis, C.S. *Mere Christianity.* New York: Macmillan, 1970.

Lyotard, Jean-François. *The Postmodern Condition: A Report on Knowledge.* Geoff Bennington and Brian Massumi, trs. Minneapolis, MN: University of Minnesota Press, 1991.

Mather, Cotton. *Magnalia Christi Americana; or, The Eccleseastical History of New England,* vol. 2, 1852. Reprint. New York: Russell & Russell, 1967.

Miller, Robert T., and Ronald B. Flowers. *Towards Benevolent Neutrality: Church, State, and the Supreme Court.* 4th ed. Waco, TX: Baylor University Press, 1992.

Murray, William J. *My Life Without God.* Eugene, OR: Harvest House, 1992.

Rice, Charles E. *The Supreme Court and Public Prayer: The Need for Restraint.* New York: Fordham University Press, 1964.

Sahakian, William S., and Mabel Lewis. *John Locke.* Boston: Twayne Publishers, 1975.

Schaeffer, Franky. *A Time for Anger: The Myth of Neutrality.* Wheaton, IL: Crossway Books, 1982.

Sommers, Christina, and Fred Sommers. *Vice and Virtue in Everyday Life: Introductory Readings in Ethics.* Fort Worth, TX: Harcourt Brace Jovanovich College Publishers, 1993.

Sowell, Thomas. *Inside American Education: The Decline, the Deception, the Dogmas.* New York: The Free Press, 1993.

Squandrito, Kathleen M. *John Locke.* Boston: Twayne Publishers, 1979.

Staver, Mathew D. *Faith and Freedom: A Complete Handbook for Defending Your Religious Rights.* Wheaton, IL: Crossway Books, 1995.

Stokes, Anson Phelps, and Leo Pfeffer. *Church and State in the United States.* New York: Harper & Row, 1964.

Straus, Oscar S. *Roger Williams: The Pioneer of Religious Liberty.* New York: D. Appleton-Century, 1936.

Tocqueville, Alexis de. *Democracy in America.* vol 1. Henry Reeve, tr. Phillips Bradley, ed. New York: Vintage Books, 1990.

Wallace, Dewey D., Jr. *The Pilgrims.* Wilmington, DE: Consortium Book, 1977.

Watts, Michael R. *The Dissenters: From the Reformation to the French Revolution.* Oxford, England: Clarendon Press, 1978.

Williams, Roger. "The Bloudy Tenet of Persecution" in *The Complete Writings of Roger Williams,* vol. 3, Samuel J. Caldwell, ed. New York: Russell & Russell, 1963.

Winthrop, John. "A Short Story of the Rise, reign, and ruin of the Antinomians, Familists & Libertines, that infected the Churches of New England..." Photocopy of original, 1644.